Thanks to Lee Gatiss and thirty-nine leadii.., scholars and pastors from around the globe, the Church Society has compiled a wonderful resource for the study of Anglicanism's defining DNA, the *Thirty-nine Articles*. Each article is treated in turn with an opening key verse of Scripture, a brief but pithy commentary reflecting both its historical context and current relevance, reflective questions and a concluding prayer. Here is the perfect resource for a daily Lenten discipline of studying the essential truths of the Reformation for Anglicanism today.

**Dr Ashley Null, German Research Council Fellow,
Humboldt University of Berlin**

Foundations of Faith is not only well prepared but highly necessary at a time when the ignorance and confusion concerning Anglicanism is tragically prevalent especially among Anglicans.

Bishop Greg Venables, Primate of the Southern Cone

What holds the Anglican Communion together is not just the scripture but a specifically Anglican understanding of how those scriptures shape the life, doctrine and worship of the Church. At a time when there is little clarity over the boundaries of our Church, this is a timely reminder of what defines the Anglican centre.

Paul Harcourt, National Leader, New Wine England

This collection of brief chapters by evangelical scholars from around the world explains the meaning and argues for the relevance of the *Thirty-nine Articles of Religion* for today. The contributions are concise, accessible and persuasive. 2017 marked the 500th anniversary of the Reformation and *Foundations of Faith* highlights the need for an ongoing reformation in the Church of England. This is essential reading if the Church of England is not to dismiss or ignore its Anglican inheritance, 'the faith uniquely revealed in the Holy Scriptures.'

Julian Henderson, Bishop of Blackburn

The *Thirty-nine Articles* of Faith which I will be more comfortable to refer to as "Thirty-Nine Articles of the Faith" is about the most profound dogmatic summary of the fundamental contents of our reasonable Faith bequeathed to us by our forebears in the common Faith. They are Bible-based and in full concord with the traditions of the Church. In this age of emergence of different gospels, which are no gospels at all, the Church needed to hear again the authentic doctrine as handed down to enable her contend for the faith once for all times delivered to the saints. We consider this book, coming after more than 500 years of the historic Reformation, as God speaking to the Church again. Without reservations, therefore, we commend and recommend this book to all Anglicans of the GAFCON family, and Christians everywhere, who yet seek after God and His Kingdom through Jesus Christ.

The Most Revd Nicholas D. Okoh,
Archbishop, Metropolitan, and Primate of All Nigeria.
Chairman, GAFCON Primates' Council

Here you will find a clear, crisp, and engaging explanation of the *Thirty-nine Articles*. If you have always meant to read them, but have never gotten around to it, this will be an immense help. If you are a teacher looking for an introduction to the foundational doctrines of Anglican Christianity, look no further, buy a big stack.

Anne Kennedy, Anglican Blogger

FOUNDATIONS OF
FAITH

REFLECTIONS ON THE
THIRTY-NINE ARTICLES

Church
Society
EQUIPPING GOD'S
PEOPLE TO LIVE
GOD'S WORD

Foundations of Faith: Reflections on the Thirty-nine Articles
Edited by Lee Gatiss

The views expressed by the authors of individual chapters in this book do not necessarily represent those of Church Society.

© Church Society/Lost Coin Books, 2018.

Published for Church Society by Lost Coin Books, London.
email: lostcoinbooks@gmail.com
web: www.lostcoinbooks.com

Church Society   LOST CIN
www.churchsociety.org
admin@churchsociety.org

Scripture references are taken from the English Standard Version (ESV) Anglicised Version, and used by kind permission of Crossway and Harper Collins.

Church Society, Ground Floor, Centre Block
Hille Business Estate, 132 St Albans Road
Watford WD24 4AE, UK
Tel +44 (0)1923 255410

ISBN 9781784983390 (Paperback)

Contents

This book is dedicated to

the Revd Dr Michael J. Ovey (1958-2017)

late Principal of Oak Hill Theological College in London and a key leader in Church Society, who taught a generation of students to trust God's unerring word and to enjoy the study of church history and doctrine so essential for ministers today.

TO INSPIRE AND TO GUIDE:

THE THIRTY-NINE ARTICLES AS OUR

INHERITANCE OF FAITH

I t is now more than 500 years since Luther's famous stand against indulgences, and the birth of the Reformation. There has been much debate about the legacy of those tumultuous days. Naturally we want to repudiate the violence of the sixteenth century, and must regret that there was and is division amongst the churches. Ultimately, however, the Reformation clarified a very necessary distinction between teaching which leads people astray spiritually and the more edifying teaching of the Bible — freshly released into the world, in a language people could understand, by the Protestant Reformers.

In this book, we will be exploring the foundational statements of Anglican teaching written by some of those Reformers. *The Thirty-nine Articles of Religion* give us some excellent doctrinal handles on the teaching of the Bible, to which of course they are themselves entirely subordinate.

Certainly the Articles were designed to be more than a historical curiosity. Some people have said that the Church of England is not a 'confessional church.' If by this it is meant that our Articles are not an exhaustive survey of all we believe on every theological topic, then it may contain some truth. But if it is taken to mean that we have no stated doctrinal foundations and confess no basic, essential truths, the formularies demonstrate otherwise. They were written around the same time as other confessions, and often borrow language from the continental texts, such as the Augsburg Confession. Canon 36 of the 1604 Canon Law laid down that all clergy should subscribe *ex animo* to the Articles, and Charles I declared that they express 'the true doctrine of the Church of England agreeable to God's word.' Though things have changed somewhat since then, the Thirty-nine Articles remain at the heart of the ecclesiastical constitution of the Church of England.

The Church of England's Canon A2 states that the Articles are 'agreeable to the Word of God and may be assented unto with a good conscience by all members of the Church of England.' We are a confessional and assenting church. Not just clergy, but all members of the Church of England ought to be able to assent to the Articles with a good conscience as expressing our confession of faith. Indeed, Canon A5 goes on to say that the doctrine of the Church of England, grounded in the Holy Scriptures, 'is to be found in the Thirty-nine Articles of Religion,' along with the Book of Common Prayer and the Ordinal. So they are a statement of official, authorised Anglican doctrine.

Despite the fact that subscription requirements have been somewhat watered down, all Church of England clergy must still refer to the Articles. In their Declaration of Assent at ordination each is asked to affirm their 'loyalty to this inheritance of faith' as their 'inspiration and guidance under God' (Canon C15). This may not be the sort of subscription that requires agreement with every single word 'without reservation', but it clearly commits any honest ordinand to a careful study of the Articles and a generally submissive and joyful demeanour towards them.

The formularies are not merely descriptive of what former generations thought: they still bind those who make such declarations with integrity; they are Anglican DNA. They can be of great use in contemporary debates and are an underemployed resource in many Anglican discussions. So I hope that you will enjoy discovering or re-discovering these important and pithy statements of biblical and Reformational teaching, and then put them to use again in your own church as appropriate.

The Thirty-nine Articles are what Jim Packer once called, 'the Church of England's theological identity-card.' In the midst of all the disagreements and debates of the Reformation, they show what it is that Anglicanism has always stood for. They outline the gospel of salvation by grace alone through faith alone which had been so powerfully rediscovered in the sixteenth century, and give a definite shape to the comprehensiveness of the Church of England.

The Articles have stood the test of time. As I have already mentioned, they remain the gold standard of Anglican faith and are accepted as the legal basis of the Church of England's doctrine. But they have also been adopted and referenced in the foundational documents of numerous provinces of the Anglican Communion around the world. They form a key part of the Jerusalem Declaration on which the GAFCON Movement has so boldly taken its stand to refresh Anglican identity amidst the challenge of liberalism (the theological cuckoo in Anglicanism's nest). 'We uphold the Thirty-nine Articles,' says the Jerusalem Declaration, 'as containing the true doctrine of the Church agreeing with God's Word and as authoritative for Anglicans today.'

So genuine Anglicanism takes its theological bearings from the Articles. Yet they are only ever a subordinate standard, under the authority (as they themselves tell us) of the Bible — the unerring word of God itself. They help us interpret the scriptures, and apply their teaching to issues of controversy which are of perennial importance.

It is the zeitgeist of the age to be anti-authoritarian and anti-institutions. In the twenty-first century, particularly in the West, we like to focus on freedom and 'doing our own thing.' This is part of the shallow immaturity of a decadent and dying culture. It is also, perhaps, one of the sinful desires of youth of which the apostle Paul wrote (2 Timothy 2:22), to reject the wisdom of the past and move the ancient boundary markers to places where we might feel more comfortable (see Proverbs 22:28). Entrepreneurial leaders with charisma, charm, and courage often want to do away with the old, and set out on novel paths to excite a new generation.

Nothing happens without energetic individuals; but nothing lasts without solid institutions. Institutions are an essential mechanism for harnessing and empowering people who want to make a lasting change without being shackled to and weakened by the eccentricities of changeable leadership. Yet institutions need solid foundations. The Thirty-nine Articles were designed to be just such a solid foundation for Anglican churches. In the stormiest seas and most treacherous conditions, they help us find our bearings, anchoring us to the glorious gospel and its ecclesiastical implications.

Well-constructed institutions with clear, public confessions of faith are ways of expressing love—love for our neighbours and love for one another in the church. Shaky foundations, dishonest subscription, or doctrinal fuzziness show a lack of care for the salvation and edification of others.

Orthodoxy is a gift from God and not a human work in which we can boast. So its long term persistence must be something which requires not only thoughtful institution building but the Spirit of God. No matter how good the confessional formulas are, we always need the ongoing grace of God. Hence the old slogan *"ecclesia reformata semper reformanda secundem verbum Dei"* — reformed churches must always be continually reformed, in accordance with the word of God.

In Cambridge, one of our libraries contains an original handwritten copy of the Articles, followed by the signatures of various sixteenth-century dignitaries. It is kept safely behind glass, as a national treasure. I once persuaded the senior librarian to take it out of its case so I could examine it in more intimate detail. That was a very stimulating experience for me as a student of Anglican history; and, I have to confess, I was very tempted to add my own name to the list of those subscribing at the end. I jokingly took out a pen, but the librarian was not amused. The book was soon safely behind glass once again.

Yet these words originally drafted by Archbishop Thomas Cranmer and others from the first generation of our Protestant Reformers, should not remain forever behind lock and key. They are freely available for us to study today. Each generation must re-examine and re-appropriate them afresh as our inspiration and guidance under scripture for life in an Anglican setting. To do that well, we must understand their background and context; but most of all we must know their content.

During Lent 2017, I gathered a stellar cast of Anglican pastors and theologians from around the world to contribute to a daily blog on the Thirty-nine Articles at churchsociety.org. Their historical, biblical, and pastoral reflections on these foundational teachings of global Anglicanism are clear and compelling. They navigate some of the difficult terrain with skill and dexterity. So this short but meaty book, which gathers together those Lenten reflections, is an excellent guide for the newcomer, and a refreshing commentary for the seasoned interpreter.

To each commentary, I have added headings, some Bible passages, discussion starters, questions for reflection, and prayers in the style of the Book of Common Prayer, so that this guide might be even more useful for individuals or groups. I am very grateful to my colleague, David Meager, and my wife, Kerry Gatiss, for their help in compiling a Scripture Index. It is my sincere prayer that you will be inspired by this collection of meditations to return to the Articles themselves, and then inspired by them to return again to the word of God, with pulse racing and heart warmed by the wonderfully applied truths of the Reformation gospel.

Soli Deo Gloria.

The Revd Dr Lee Gatiss (editor) is Director of Church Society and co-author of *Be Faithful: Remaining Steadfast in the Church of England Today,* and *Reformed Foundations, Reforming Future: A Vision for 21st Century Anglicans.* He lives in Cambridge, England with his wife, Kerry, and their 3 children, and has been an ordained Church of England minister for 17 years.

BIBLE READING

Isaiah 40:12-18

Who has measured the waters in the hollow of his hand
    and marked off the heavens with a span,
enclosed the dust of the earth in a measure
    and weighed the mountains in scales
    and the hills in a balance?
Who has measured the Spirit of the LORD,
    or what man shows him his counsel?
Whom did he consult,
    and who made him understand?
 Who taught him the path of justice,
    and taught him knowledge,
    and showed him the way of understanding?
Behold, the nations are like a drop from a bucket,
    and are accounted as the dust on the scales;
    behold, he takes up the coastlands like fine dust.
Lebanon would not suffice for fuel,
    nor are its beasts enough for a burnt offering.
All the nations are as nothing before him,
    they are accounted by him as less than nothing and empti-
    ness.
To whom then will you liken God,
    or what likeness compare with him?

STARTER QUESTION

Why is it so difficult to find something to compare God to?

ARTICLE I

OF FAITH IN
THE HOLY TRINITY

~

There is but one living and true God,
everlasting, without body, parts, or
passions; of infinite power, wisdom,
and goodness; the Maker, and Preserver
of all things both visible and invisible.
And in unity of this Godhead there be
three Persons, of one substance, power,
and eternity; the Father, the Son, and
the Holy Ghost.

ARTICLE I

To be Protestant, we need to be *catholic*. That's the key point of Article I, and the sure foundation upon which all the Articles are built.

Hang on though, you might say—wasn't the Reformation about being against Catholicism, about refuting its many errors?

But here's the thing — the Protestant Reformers were so opposed to the Roman Catholic Church because they saw that it had ceased to be truly catholic. The word 'catholic' means 'universal' — so to be 'catholic' means to believe what the Church has always believed. That's what we're affirming in the Apostles' Creed when we say that we believe in 'the holy catholic church.'

By the sixteenth century, the Church of Rome had deviated so far from the truths revealed in Scripture, that it could no longer be properly recognised as 'catholic' any more. It was the Protestants who were the true catholics—they weren't breaking away from the church, they were returning to it.

And so when the Anglican Reformers came to write the Articles, they made this conviction dramatically clear. They were going 'back to basics' — back to the true faith, the uncorrupted faith, the faith authoritatively proclaimed in God's word, the faith articulated by the church's great champions of orthodoxy.

That's why the Thirty-nine Articles don't kick off with a 'hot potato' issue of their day (like the role of the Pope), but by going back to the most central of all Christian beliefs: that there is one God, who is Father, Son, and Holy Spirit.

The Incomparable God

It's easy for the doctrine of the Trinity to appear rather arcane, or even irrelevant to us. Isn't it the kind of thing that's great for keeping academic theologians in a job, but which has precious little to offer to the ordinary believer in the pew?

Well, it's certainly true that Article 1 is rigorously and richly theological—it breathes the air of centuries of studious reflection on the biblical witness to the nature of God. Anglicans can have confidence here—what we believe wasn't jotted down in a hurry on the back of a postcard, but handed down carefully across many hundreds of years.

In fact, good theology is not the enemy of pastoral relevance, but its necessary precondition. Article 1 is, indeed, supremely practical. Look at the God it's inviting us to worship.

Here is a God utterly unlike me. I'm mortal, he's everlasting; I'm physical, he's 'without body'; I'm at the whim of my emotional ups and downs; he's without passions. And the list goes on: I'm frequently powerless, he possesses 'infinite power'; I'm frequently stupid, he's perfectly wise; I'm frequently sinful, he is 'goodness' itself.

This relentless 'distancing' of God's nature and character from ours is, perhaps paradoxically, profoundly consoling. I'm not putting my faith in another 'creature', or a bigger 'Me' in the sky, a mere projection of my own failings and hang-ups. The God revealed in the Bible, and affirmed in Article 1, is alone Creator ('the maker and preserver of all things')—and that means that he stands outside and above everything else.

The God who governs the cosmos, who numbers every hair on my head, is perfectly good and perfectly wise—so he knows what he's doing with my life. The God who holds the universe in being, and who gives me my every breath, is fully present to me at every moment, even when I'm feeling abandoned or alone. The God who is eternal, who is Life itself, can alone offer me true hope in the face of my own death, and amid the shadow of the grave.

THE GLORIOUS TRINITY

But there's still more to say, because this one God is 'three Persons, of one substance, power and eternity.' God is not a lonely monad, reliant on his creation to enable him to relate and to love. God is relationship, God is love. He is the eternal, loving, joyful communion of Father, Son, and Holy Spirit. In other words, God doesn't need me in order to be himself—before anything existed, he loved.

That too is wonderful, liberating news for us to hear. Because it means that God doesn't create me as a part of a deal he struck, or relate to me on the basis of *quid pro quo*. It means that the salvation he offers doesn't depend on me fulfilling certain requirements, but can be received by me freely as a pure gift, no strings attached. It is a salvation given by grace alone, through faith alone.

And that's a truth that the Anglican Reformers especially wanted to recover. That's why they went 'back to basics' in Article 1, back to the Trinity, back to God himself. Because they knew that to be Protestant, we need to be catholic.

The Revd Dr Mark Smith *is the Chaplain of Christ's College, Cambridge, teaches early church history in the Faculty of Divinity at Cambridge, and is Review Editor of Churchman.*

QUESTIONS FOR REFLECTION

1. Why is it so important to be properly catholic in our under-standing of God?
2. Why is it so crucial for our faith that God is not like us?
3. How Trinitarian is your everyday expression of faith?

PRAYER

Almighty and everlasting God, you have given us grace to bear witness to the glory of the eternal Trinity and to worship you alone: keep us firm in the confession of this faith and defend us in your mighty power, for you live and reign—the one true God—Father, Son, and Holy Spirit. *Amen.*

BIBLE READING

Hebrews 2:14-18

Since therefore the children share in flesh and blood, he himself likewise partook of the same things, that through death he might destroy the one who has the power of death, that is, the devil, and deliver all those who through fear of death were subject to lifelong slavery. For surely it is not angels that he helps, but he helps the offspring of Abraham. Therefore he had to be made like his brothers in every respect, so that he might become a merciful and faithful high priest in the service of God, to make propitiation for the sins of the people. For because he himself has suffered when tempted, he is able to help those who are being tempted.

STARTER QUESTION

Why did God become a man?

ARTICLE II

OF THE WORD OR SON OF GOD, WHICH WAS MADE VERY MAN

~

The Son, which is the Word of the Father, begotten from everlasting of the Father, the very and eternal God, and of one substance with the Father, took man's nature in the womb of the Blessed Virgin, of her substance: so that two whole and perfect natures, that is to say the Godhead and manhood, were joined together in one Person, never to be divided, whereof is one Christ, very God and very Man, who truly suffered, was crucified, dead and buried, to reconcile his Father to us and to be a sacrifice, not only for original guilt but also for all actual sins of men.

ARTICLE II

C hristianity is uniquely distinguished from any other faith, not only in its teaching about the Trinity articulated in Article 1, but particularly in understanding the person and work of Jesus Christ, who is the subject of Article 2.

Historically, this Article substantially reproduces the 3rd Article of the Augsburg Confession of 1530. Only in its last phrase, referring to the atonement, does it address an area of controversy with respect to Roman Catholicism. In its historical context it was more concerned to articulate the universally agreed creedal truths about Jesus over and against some Anabaptist revisiting of ancient heresies.

What is essential for us to know about Jesus Christ, according to the Article? Three things: how he is truly God; how he is also truly human; and how he is our Saviour.

TRUE GOD

Jesus is truly God because his essence or substance is divine. He has a whole and perfect divine nature. Yet, although complete in his Godhead, he is in eternal and perfect relationship with the Father. He is begotten from everlasting; this is his 'eternal generation', which means that he is wholly God and yet distinguishable in relation to the Father, as a Son.

Sonship here emphasises, not that he was 'birthed' in time by the Father—which is the ancient heresy of Arius against which the Nicene Creed was written in 325AD—but rather that he is God in the same way that the Father is God. Neither does Jesus' Sonship imply that he is inferior to the Father; the analogy of the order of Father and Son is not something constraining the Son in relation to the Father, but is the free and eternal expression of their relationship in the Trinity. We are only aware of this relationship because, as the 'Word' of the Father, the Son perfectly and completely expresses the one will and revealed purpose of God.

TRUE HUMAN
For human beings to be able to be in a real personal relationship to this living God, it is necessary that Jesus is also truly human. Jesus became wholly and perfectly human by incarnation, by a miraculous conception in the womb of a virgin (by which she was 'blessed'). He thereby acquired an essence or substance that is really, wholly, and perfectly human. By incarnation, two whole and perfect natures came together in one Person. This understanding was the fruit of centuries of reflection by the church, expressed in the Article.

The Son is 'very God' (i.e. truly God). Arius denied this in 325, but a divine creature would not be worthy of worship nor a true revealer of God.

The Son is 'very Man.' This is asserted against the Apollinarian heresy (c. 360) which denied Christ's true humanity by saying he was only a divine mind in a human body—which made the righteousness of his life irrelevant to us and fruitless for us to follow.

The Son is 'one Person, never to be divided'—declared against Nestorianism in 431, which denied the unity of the Person of Christ, saying he was two persons united in a 'marriage' of sorts—which would mean that Jesus' humanity becomes only a good human example to us, not a divine revelation.

The Son is 'one Christ, very God and very Man'—said against Eutychianism in 451 which denied the distinction of the two natures of Christ—which would have meant Jesus had a different sort of nature to ours and thereby would be unable to take our place in the atonement.

TRUE SAVIOUR

Having established Jesus' perfect divinity and humanity, the Article summarises how he is uniquely and perfectly the Saviour of his people. Salvation is first rooted in the real historical events of Jesus' crucifixion and death. In his human nature, Jesus 'truly suffered, was crucified, dead and buried', against Docetic heresies that said it only seemed that way.

Jesus' resurrection is affirmed later in Article 4, but Article 2 establishes that the climax of the work of Christ is in his death, which reveals the great depth of his love for his people. Jesus' death primarily achieves two things: reconciliation and atonement. Jesus' purpose in dying was 'to reconcile his Father to us', which is an unusual phrase, as Scripture more commonly talks of us being reconciled to God. However the Article establishes the point that our real problem, for which Jesus died, is not in us—that we have fallen out with God—but rather that our sinfulness deserves God's righteous anger, and only the death penalty will satisfy our violation of his holiness.

That is why Jesus is our Saviour by being 'a sacrifice.' A suitable, perfect sacrifice dying in our place—a substitutionary atonement—satisfies God's justice not only for 'original guilt' (which is the same as 'original sin' seen from God's perspective), but also our 'actual sins.' This last reference is specifically addressed against the Roman Catholic view that while Jesus's death dealt with original sin, it required the sacrifices of Masses to deal with our actual sins. However, the Article implies Jesus's one perfect sacrifice is sufficient in itself to atone. This also underlines that Jesus' atonement does more than make salvation a potential for anyone to tap into; rather it dealt with our specific real and actual sins—his atonement is objective and definite.

In summary, Jesus Christ is unique. There is no other person who is both perfectly God and perfectly human, and thereby able to truly reveal God to us and able to identify wholly with us. Only he can be a Mediator between us and God (Article 7). He alone thereby is qualified to be the sacrifice that atones for our sins, bringing us reconciliation and forgiveness.

The Article establishes how the slogan is true:

NO CHRIST = NO GOD;
KNOW CHRIST = KNOW GOD.

The Revd Dr Rob Munro *is the Rector of St Mary's Cheadle, Rural Dean of Cheadle, and Chairman of the Council of the Fellowship of Word and Spirit.*

Questions for Reflection

1. Why could we only be saved by God himself?
2. Why is it important to insist on the true human nature of Christ?
3. Do you speak about Christ's sacrifice the way Article 2 does?

Prayer

Almighty Father, who gave us your only Son to take our nature upon him and to be born of the virgin Mary: grant that we, being saved from your wrath by his perfect sacrifice may be daily renewed in his image, to the glory of your name. *Amen.*

Bible Reading

Acts 2:25-32

David says concerning him,

"I saw the Lord always before me,
    for he is at my right hand that I may not be shaken;
    therefore my heart was glad, and my tongue rejoiced;
    my flesh also will dwell in hope.
For you will not abandon my soul to Hades,
    or let your Holy One see corruption.
You have made known to me the paths of life;
    you will make me full of gladness with your presence.'

'Brothers, I may say to you with confidence about the patriarch David that he both died and was buried, and his tomb is with us to this day. Being therefore a prophet, and knowing that God had sworn with an oath to him that he would set one of his descendants on his throne, he foresaw and spoke about the resurrection of the Christ, that he was not abandoned to Hades, nor did his flesh see corruption. This Jesus God raised up, and of that we all are witnesses.

Starter Question

What do you think Jesus was doing the day after Good Friday?

ARTICLE III

OF THE GOING DOWN OF CHRIST INTO HELL

~

As Christ died for us, and was buried,
so also it is to be believed, that he went
down into Hell.

ARTICLE III

Article 3 is the shortest but, at the time they were written, one of the most controverted of the Thirty-nine Articles. Debates on the continent spilled over to England, where, amongst others, the Marian exiles who had spent time in Geneva began to champion the Swiss reformers' understanding that this was an important Article that helped us understand the fullness of what Christ suffered on the cross.

The version of this Article that was approved in 1563 and published in 1571 was shorter than the same Article as it had appeared in 1553. A further sentence which referenced 1 Peter 3 and spoke of Christ's spirit being present with the spirits in prison and preaching to them was removed, it seems, on the floor of the English convocation of bishops. This had the effect of presenting the *fact* of Christ's presence among the dead without providing an *explanation*.

HELL?

One of the difficulties then and now with this Article has been the use of the word 'hell.' The original Anglo-Saxon word simply meant 'covered' or 'unseen.' It referred to a realm that was beyond human perception. In this way, it echoed the Greek word *hades* or the Hebrew word *sheol* that spoke of the realm of the departed. However, by the time of the Reformation the word had narrowed its meaning to the place where the unrepentant wicked experience the judgment and wrath of God. This reality had been designated by a very different Greek word, Gehenna.

So one of the big questions surrounding this Article and the Article from the Apostles' Creed which it reflects, is whether the word used designates the place of the dead or the place of torment and judgment. It would seem that in 1563 the Convocation was content to leave all options open.

Not quite all. It is clear from the draft papers that Thomas Cranmer and his successors wanted to avoid any suggestion of purgatory or a second chance for conversion after death. Cranmer's original line to that effect was probably dropped because the subject would be dealt with in a later Article (Article 22).

Is this Biblical?

The most important question concerning this Article is the question of its biblical warrant. Is it really what the Bible teaches? Those who have spoken about it (and the clause from the Apostles' Creed) have in fact appealed to quite an array of biblical passages to provide a ground for talking like this.

a. The words of David in Psalm 16:10, taken up by Peter in Acts 2:27, 31 and applied to Jesus: 'You will not abandon my soul to Sheol, or let your holy one see corruption.' He was in Sheol but he was not abandoned there.

b. Jonah, the only Old Testament prophet to whom the Lord compares himself, experienced judgment in order to save the lives of others. 'For just as Jonah was three days and three nights in the belly of the great fish', Jesus said, 'so will the Son of Man be three days and three nights in the heart of the earth' (Matthew 12:40).

c. In Matthew 12:29, in answer to the blasphemy of the Jewish leaders, Jesus asked 'Or how can someone enter a strong man's house and plunder his goods, unless he first binds the strong man? Then indeed he may plunder his house' (Matthew 12:29). Some Lutherans tended to favour this as an explanation of what happened when Jesus 'descended into hell.'

d. Romans 10:5–7 speaks of not needing to ascend to heaven to bring Christ down or descending to the abyss in order to bring Christ up from the dead. It is part of a larger argument but assumes that at one point he was among the dead, though he is no longer there. He does not need to be brought back because he has been raised from the dead.

e. Ephesians 4, and in particular Paul's explanation of Psalm 68:18, involves the expression 'he descended to the lower parts of the earth.' While some have taken this as simply a reference to the incarnation, why did Paul use this expression if all he meant was 'the earth'?

f. Colossians 2:15 speaks of how Christ 'disarmed the rulers and authorities and put them to open shame, by triumphing over them in the cross'. In the context, though, it is clear that what Paul has in mind is the triumph of the cross itself and not some subsequent activity.

g. The most often quoted text in this connection is 1 Peter 3:18–20, the text referred to in the Forty-Two Articles (1553). The text contains a number of unanswered questions (when did Christ preach to the people of Noah's day? Through Noah at the time of the Flood or after the crucifixion? What was the purpose of that preaching? To save or to announce his triumph?). However, in its context this is an illustration intended as an encouragement to persevere in suffering because Christ suffered 'once for all' in order to save us.

h. Revelation 1:18 contains the words of the glorious risen Christ: 'Fear not, I am the first and the last, and the living one. I died, and behold I am alive forevermore, and I have the keys of Death and Hades.' It is a message of complete and utter triumph over the last great enemy of men and women. Death has been defeated, completely emptied of all power.

The idea of Christ's descent to hell, however it might be explained, is based on the cumulative evidence of biblical testimony like this. Perhaps it is ultimately unhelpful to anchor it in any one of these passages but we should rather see it arising as part of the biblical theological movement from promise to fulfilment. The great curse that entered human experience after the Fall—death and the right and perfect judgment of a holy God—has finally been overcome by the one who himself experienced it in all its fullness. There is not one aspect of death as we experience it that he did not share in order to triumph over it. As one writer deftly put it, 'Death has no mystery which He did not fathom' (A. J. Tait).

Does it Matter?

What then is the theological and practical import of this doctrine? In outline, we must say:

1. There is no second chance on the other side of the grave. Nothing in the Bible suggests anything like post-mortem repentance or post-mortem faith. It is our response to the gospel in this life which determines our destiny, a response entirely enabled by the work of God's Spirit in us. There is no license here for a probationary hell, purgatory, or a second chance.

2. The death and resurrection of Jesus is the ground of our personal salvation but also much more than that. There is no part of creation that remains untouched by what God has done in Christ. The cross changes everything and by the power of what Jesus accomplished there, the principalities and powers are disarmed and we have nothing to fear (Colossians 2:15).

3. The cross is sufficient. From the cross Jesus said 'It is finished' (John 19:30). Jesus bore all the physical and spiritual dimensions of the curse against sin on the cross. It does not need to be supplemented because it is a complete redemption.

4. The descent into hell is not something added to the cross (he died and he descended into hell) but instead a theological perspective on the cross. Jesus bore death for us as a physical and spiritual reality. He bore the whole thing, not just the dimensions we can witness from this side of the experience. He drank the cup

of God's wrath to the dregs.

5. The descent into hell helps us understand the resurrection as well. It was a real resurrection and not simply a resuscitation. He was raised out of the fullness of the judgment he took upon himself for us.

6. The descent into hell helps us to see the extent of God's action to save us. He did not deal with our guilt and corruption and alienation from him and enslavement to sin in a superficial way. In the weakness and humiliation of the cross, the sovereign God triumphed over it all and has left no aspect of it intact. God is completely and utterly our Saviour.

7. The descent into hell is a richly comforting doctrine for Christian men and women. There is no aspect of what faces us that he has not experienced and emptied of power. Those who belong to Jesus have absolutely nothing to fear. Jesus has the keys of death and Hades.

The Revd Dr Mark D. Thompson *is the Principal of Moore Theological College, Sydney and author of 'The Origin of the Thirty-nine Articles' and 'The History of Subscription to the Thirty-Nine Articles' in Churchman 125 (2011).*

QUESTIONS FOR REFLECTION

1. Why is it important that Jesus really did die, and not just appear to die?
2. How does this Article help us understand the resurrection better?
3. How does this Article comfort and encourage believers?

PRAYER

Almighty God, look with mercy upon your family, for which our Lord Jesus Christ suffered death upon the cross: grant that we may continually put to death our sinful desires and be buried with him, so that we may pass through the grave and gate of death to our joyful resurrection, through Jesus Christ our Saviour. *Amen.*

Bible Reading

1 Corinthians 15:12-19

Now if Christ is proclaimed as raised from the dead, how can some of you say that there is no resurrection of the dead? But if there is no resurrection of the dead, then not even Christ has been raised. And if Christ has not been raised, then our preaching is in vain and your faith is in vain. We are even found to be misrepresenting God, because we testified about God that he raised Christ, whom he did not raise if it is true that the dead are not raised. For if the dead are not raised, not even Christ has been raised. And if Christ has not been raised, your faith is futile and you are still in your sins. Then those also who have fallen asleep in Christ have perished. If in Christ we have hope in this life only, we are of all people most to be pitied.

Starter Question

What would you do if archaeologists discovered the body of Jesus?

ARTICLE IV

OF THE RESURRECTION OF CHRIST

~

Christ did truly rise again from death,
and took again his body, with flesh,
bones, and all things appertaining
to the perfection of Man's nature;
wherewith he ascended into Heaven,
and there sitteth, until he return to
judge all Men at the last day.

ARTICLE IV

'Why was Jesus raised from the dead?', I have sometimes heard Christians ask. 'I understand that he died for our sins—he paid the penalty, he took my punishment. That I understand. But he said on the cross that it is finished. So why did he have to rise again?'

It's a good question, and shows the need for proper doctrinal understanding to put the different parts of God's story together theologically. The answer I've often heard given to these enquiring Christians isn't bad, but could be better. 'If Jesus didn't rise,' the answer goes, 'how would we know that it worked?'

As far as it goes, this answer is accurate. It is true that by raising him from the dead, God vindicates Jesus, declares that his wrath has indeed been satisfied, that Jesus has truly paid for the sins that he bore although he had no sin of his own. But the resurrection is about much more than just *knowledge*.

WHAT DID THE RESURRECTION ACHIEVE?

Jesus was raised to life for our justification, Romans 4:25 tells us. Jesus *is* the resurrection, as he told Martha in John 11; with him has started the resurrection age that the Old Testament looked forward to at the end of time. His resurrection causes us to be born again to a living hope, we know from 1 Peter 1. Now resurrected, Jesus lives for eternity in right relationship with God; as we live in faith-union with Jesus, we share in that right relationship, enjoying our justification now. Yes, with his death, it was finished, in that the propitiatory sacrifice for sin was made; but in his resurrection, his perfect righteousness brings us with him into the very throne room of God. There is no condemnation for us, because he lives, interceding for us before God.

The resurrection is a doctrinally rich topic. Jesus' resurrection is inextricably linked to his judgment, as Paul tells us in Acts 17:31: 'God has fixed a day on which he will judge the world by the man he has appointed, and he has given assurance of this by raising that man from the dead.'

Soon Jesus will return. We are almost there. We suffer trials as we wait; but they will be nothing compared to the glory that is about to come. There will be injustice as we struggle to live out our days in this fallen world which is hostile to Christ. But the saints will be vindicated. Jesus is coming in judgment, and every knee will bow—some joyfully, many reluctantly, but there will be no doubt of his lordship then.

The Physical Defeat of Death

Article 4 also reminds us that the resurrection is physical; Jesus' resurrection was real and actually happened. His body was dead, and then it was alive. Jesus came back from the dead in a renewed and marvellous human body, and so will we. Christians are pro-matter. We believe the physical creation is good, and we do not aim to escape it or transcend it. The new creation will be better, freed from its frustration, but it will still be physical, and we will have physical bodies in it. We do not look forward to an ethereal existence, disembodied consciousness in communion with God, but to eternal resurrected bodies living in a physical world.

Jesus' resurrection is the demonstration of the defeat of death, which has held all humanity in fear since Adam's sin. We need not fear death when we are in Christ, for just as he was raised from the dead, we will also be raised. Death and its related decay will not be part of the new creation; the sources of tears that are so frequent in this world will be done away with.

This means that the resurrection is our hope. We do not mourn as the pagans do, wondering if death is the end, and never knowing for sure what might lie after it. We know that Christ rose as the first-fruits from the dead, and therefore so shall we who are in Christ. The resurrection age has begun, ushered in by Jesus' resurrection. The last days are here.

A Doctrine for the Present

So it matters how we live now. It matters that people come to repentance so they will meet him as Saviour, not enemy. It matters that we live in the light of the end, bringing the good news about how to escape judgment and glorifying God in our lives. Christ was raised so that we might walk in newness of life; so we should not let sin reign in our mortal bodies (Romans 6:12). The end is near, so we should be self-controlled and sober-minded for the sake of our prayers, loving one another (1 Peter 4:7). Jesus will return and transform our bodies to be like his glorious body, so we should stand firm in the Lord (Philippians 4:1).

The resurrection is not a doctrine just for the future: Jesus' resurrection and return in judgment is something that should guide our every moment, as we live day by day, making decisions to do his will rather than ours, loving one another, showing hospitality, disciplining sin and contending for the gospel. The resurrection means that, in the midst of pain and death, we rejoice. We always have reason for rejoicing. Death will soon be no more.

The Revd Dr Kirsty Birkett *teaches Ethics, Philosophy, and Church History at Oak Hill Theological College, London and is the author of The Essence of the Reformation.*

QUESTIONS FOR REFLECTION

1. What difference would it make if Jesus's resurrection was not physical?
2. Why is it important to mention the resurrection and not just the cross, in our preaching?
3. Why does the Article add that Jesus is sitting in heaven until the day he returns?

PRAYER

Almighty God, through your only Son you have conquered death and opened to us the gate of everlasting life: help us to set our minds on things above, not the fading things of this world, through Jesus Christ our Lord, who lives and reigns with you and the Holy Spirit, one God, for ever and ever. *Amen.*

Bible Reading

John 14:16-21, 25-26

I will ask the Father, and he will give you another Helper, to be with you forever, even the Spirit of truth, whom the world cannot receive, because it neither sees him nor knows him. You know him, for he dwells with you and will be in you.

I will not leave you as orphans; I will come to you. Yet a little while and the world will see me no more, but you will see me. Because I live, you also will live. In that day you will know that I am in my Father, and you in me, and I in you. Whoever has my commandments and keeps them, he it is who loves me. And he who loves me will be loved by my Father, and I will love him and manifest myself to him.

… These things I have spoken to you while I am still with you. But the Helper, the Holy Spirit, whom the Father will send in my name, he will teach you all things and bring to your remembrance all that I have said to you.

Starter Question

*Is the Holy Spirit an impersonal force
or power at work in the world?*

ARTICLE V

OF THE HOLY GHOST

~

The Holy Ghost, proceeding from the Father and the Son, is of one substance, majesty, and glory, with the Father and the Son, very and eternal God.

ARTICLE V

It is perhaps ironic that an Article which was only added by Archbishop Matthew Parker in 1563—seemingly as an afterthought to make the Articles dealing with the Trinity balance out—is today one of the most controversial. He didn't even come up with something original and instead simply copied from the Württemberg Confession of 1552.

THE *FILIOQUE* CONTROVERSY

The most controversial aspect of this Article is not what I want to focus on—but something must be said about it. The controversy is that it says the Holy Spirit proceeds from the Father *and the Son* (*filioque* in Latin). This is certainly the Anglican stance given that it is not only mentioned here but is also found in both the Athanasian Creed and *Book of Common Prayer* version of the Nicene Creed (which, as Article 8 makes clear, contain the teaching of the Bible).

In the West this short phrase 'and the Son' has not been controversial since the eleventh century and most accepted it long before then. In the East, this phrase was never accepted and continues to cause strain in the relations between our churches. The arguments and debates are fascinating to read (though not always edifying!).

Perhaps the best way to bridge this divide is to accept the understanding promoted by the Council of Florence (1439)—which the Anglican church has never renounced—that the Holy Spirit proceeds from the Father *through* the Son. This keeps the primacy of the Father which is so important to the East but also makes sense of the Bible passages referring to the relationship between the Spirit and Son.

To many, such debates are rather philosophical and academic. Whilst undoubtedly interesting and important, let us move on to the real meat of the Article.

The Divine Spirit

The most important part of this Article is that the person of the Holy Spirit is 'of one substance, majesty, and glory, with the Father and the Son, very and eternal God.' Whilst this should not be controversial, sadly, it is. The number of people in our churches who fail to grasp the most basic of beliefs about the Holy Spirit is quite frightening.

I will never forget my horror when, at college, a student who was training for ministry was surprised to be told that the Holy Spirit was a person and not just a power of some kind. A year later, sat around the table at an Easter retreat, another friend from a very different wing of the church expressed the belief that the Holy Spirit was something akin to the candle lighter the Father and the Son used in the world. In a completely different church I have heard a pastor refer to the Holy Spirit as some kind of currency the Father gives to his children to use in the world.

Let us be clear: the Holy Spirit is truly and fully God. He is as much God as Jesus or the Father. He is as glorious and majestic as the Father or the Son—indeed they share one majestic glory. The Holy Spirit is eternal and he is God. The Holy Spirit is not some Star Wars-esque 'force' or merely the power of God, and he is certainly not some divine miniature flamethrower or magical pound coin! He is the third person of the Trinity.

THE PERSONAL SPIRIT

That the Holy Spirit is a 'person' is clear in Scripture. Firstly, the titles given to him are personal: He is the Comforter and the Advocate—indeed he is 'another advocate' (John 14:16) like Jesus showing the Spirit is a person like Jesus is. Furthermore, he 'intercedes' for Christians (Romans 8:26-27) and can be personally 'grieved' (Ephesians 4:30). He has a 'will' (1 Corinthians 12:4-11) and 'leads' believers (Galatians 5:18). You can have 'fellowship' with him (2 Corinthians 13:14) and you can lie to him (Acts 5:3). He speaks and sets people apart for ministry (Acts 13:2) and then he sends them out (Acts 13:4).

All of this radically points away from an emotionless force or mere expression of divine will and towards a personable person, a relatable revelation, and an emotional emissary. This is someone you can have a very real relationship with—one which is just as rich, active, and varied as the relationships we have with the Father and the Son.

THE SPIRIT TODAY

As Christians it is absolutely vital we capture this vision and seek not only the gifts he offers us but also simply seek the Spirit as he is, for who he is. When we know the Spirit and relate to him, we will find he points us to Jesus in the most beautiful ways imaginable and turns our discipleship upside down with his grace and power.

A large part of the reason I would personally identify as a 'Charismatic' Anglican is because of the wonderful things Scripture says of the Spirit and our need for a relationship with him. It is a sad and tragic irony that such a biblical passion has often led to Christians obsessing over the gifts of the Spirit rather than seeking him, and in doing so taking their eyes off Jesus. It is important to recognise that the Holy Spirit is the Humble Spirit who always points us to Jesus and his sacrifice on Calvary. Even his gifts are given to help us know and proclaim Jesus to each other and the world.

It is good that Archbishop Parker added this to the Thirty-nine Articles. Too often the Holy Spirit is sidelined or given a few words and nothing more. To have a whole Article dedicated to his majesty and glory is a wonderful thing. This may be the second shortest of the all the Articles but it is no less important for the brevity. Amongst all the other key doctrines and teachings of our confession let us daily ensure we never lose sight of the glory, the majesty, and the divinity of the Person of the Holy Spirit.

The Revd Adam Young *is a minister in the Diocese of York.*

Questions for reflection

1. Is the Holy Spirit something within Christians which we 'use'?
2. Why do Christians often speak more about the gifts of the Spirit than about his deity?
3. How can we tell if the Spirit is active in our churches?

Prayer

Lord Jesus Christ, who taught the hearts of your faithful apostles by sending to them your Holy Spirit: grant
that by that same Spirit we may please and follow you,
to the glory of our heavenly Father. *Amen.*

BIBLE READING

2 Timothy 3:12-17

Indeed, all who desire to live a godly life in Christ Jesus will be persecuted, while evil people and impostors will go on from bad to worse, deceiving and being deceived. But as for you, continue in what you have learned and have firmly believed, knowing from whom you learned it and how from childhood you have been acquainted with the sacred writings, which are able to make you wise for salvation through faith in Christ Jesus. All Scripture is breathed out by God and profitable for teaching, for reproof, for correction, and for training in righteousness, that the man of God may be complete, equipped for every good work.

STARTER QUESTION

What is the point of the Bible?

ARTICLE VI

OF THE SUFFICIENCY OF THE HOLY SCRIPTURES FOR SALVATION

Holy Scripture containeth all things necessary
to salvation: so that whatsoever is not read
therein, nor may be proved thereby, is not
to be required of any man, that it should
be believed as an Article of the Faith, or be
thought requisite or necessary to salvation.
In the name of the holy Scripture we do
understand those Canonical Books of the Old
and New Testament, of whose authority was
never any doubt in the Church.

Of the Names and Number of the Canonical
Books:

Genesis

Exodus

Leviticus

Numbers

Deuteronomy

Joshua

Judges

Ruth

The First Book of Samuel

The Second Book of Samuel

The First Book of Kings

The Second Book of Kings

The First Book of Chronicles

The Second Book of Chronicles

The First Book of Esdras [Ezra]

The Second Book of Esdras [Nehemiah]

The Book of Esther

The Book of Job

The Psalms

The Proverbs

Ecclesiastes or Preacher

Cantica, or Songs of Solomon

Four Prophets the greater

Twelve Prophets the less

And the other Books (as Hierome saith) the
Church doth read for example of life and
instruction of manners; but yet doth it not apply
them to establish any doctrine; such are these
following:
The Third Book of Esdras
The Fourth Book of Esdras
The Book of Tobias
The Book of Judith
The rest of the Book of Esther
The Book of Wisdom
Jesus the Son of Sirach
Baruch the Prophet
The Song of the Three Children
The Story of Susanna
Of Bel and the Dragon
The Prayer of Manasses
The First Book of Maccabees
The Second Book of Maccabees

All the Books of the New Testament, as they are
commonly received, we do receive, and account
them Canonical.

Article VI

'Yes, Scripture is God's word but we cannot as Christians do without the insights of modern science and recent medical advances.'

Have you ever heard these kinds of statements? They focus on what Article 6 addresses: the sufficiency of Scripture. The first five of the Thirty-nine Articles reaffirmed the Church's universal beliefs. Article 6 now turns to issues of controversy, particularly with medieval Catholicism.

The Sufficiency of Scripture

For what is Scripture sufficient? This is the critical question because there are many issues the Bible does not address, such as the nature of quantum physics, the fundamentals of genetics, or the complexities of the human brain. Article 6 clearly states how the Bible is sufficient: 'Holy Scripture containeth all things necessary to salvation.' Scripture's purpose is to bring about people's salvation. It is not necessarily to explain the intricacies of DNA, or provide a cure for cancer.

Now, 'salvation' in Article 6 is not simply becoming a Christian. For the Reformers it also entailed perseverance until final salvation on judgment day. In short, Scripture is sufficient for both the conversion and conservation of believers.

Why did Scripture's sufficiency need affirmation in the sixteenth century? Because many in medieval Catholicism maintained that Scripture lacked knowledge necessary for salvation. They held that Jesus handed onto the church other teachings and rituals not found in Scripture. Various medieval theologians argued that these unwritten traditions had been preserved by the Holy Spirit through a continual succession of bishops passing them on through time. As John Eck, the fierce opponent of Martin Luther said in his *Handbook of Commonplaces against Martin Luther*, Christ's apostles 'taught many more things than they wrote, which have equal authority with those things written.'

The Roman Catholic Council of Trent officially decreed the insufficiency of Scripture. It insisted that the church's 'truth and discipline are contained in the written books, and the unwritten traditions which, received by the apostles from the mouth of Christ himself, or from the apostles themselves, the Holy Ghost dictating, have come down even unto us, transmitted as it were from hand to hand' (Session 4, 1546).

What were examples of these unwritten traditions? Doctrines like the perpetual virginity of Mary and rituals like the need to face East in a church service or make the sign of the cross.

The reformers admitted that Jesus himself did and said many more things not found in Scripture. But that was not the issue. It was whether what was written in the Bible was adequate for salvation. And the verses to which the reformers appealed were John 20:30–31: 'Jesus performed many other signs in the presence of his disciples, which are not recorded in this book. But these are written that you may believe that Jesus is the Messiah, the Son of God, and that by believing you may have life in his name.'

What is written in John's Gospel (which also assumes the authority of the Old Testament) is sufficient for salvation. And with every New Testament book added to this, the Bible only becomes more sufficient.

So, if Scripture is sufficient for salvation, Article 6 draws out the obvious implications: 'so that whatsoever is not read therein, nor may be proved thereby, is not to be required of any man, that it should be believed as an Article of the Faith, or be thought requisite or necessary to salvation.'

Here Article 6 unmistakably rejected any need for extra-biblical traditions in a person's salvation. It released the believer from the burden of a legion of ceremonies which had accumulated by the sixteenth century. Moreover, as the Reformers noted, it would be impossible to prove these oral traditions came from the apostles.

THE SIZE OF SCRIPTURE

If Scripture is sufficient the next obvious questions arises: which Bible do we mean? The medieval church inherited a disagreement from the early church about the number of books in Scripture. The twenty-seven New Testament books were not in doubt but there was a question about the Old Testament. It was originally written in Hebrew (with some chapters in Aramaic). However, several centuries before Christ the Old Testament was translated into Greek. This was understandable given that many scattered Jews lived outside of Israel and were raised in a world that spoke Greek. Legend had it that seventy or perhaps seventy-two people translated the Old Testament separately into Greek, and then discovered their translations were identical. Hard evidence shows this story is highly likely a myth. But in light of it, the Greek Old Testament came to be known as the Septuagint.

Now the Septuagint that circulated amidst the early church contained a collection of extra books not found in the Hebrew Old Testament. They became known as the apocrypha. What was the status of these books? On the one hand, Augustine (354-430) thought these extra books were inspired Scripture, because he believed the story of the seventy translators and that such a miracle proved the Septuagint was God-breathed (City of God, XVIII.42-43). On the other hand, the renowned linguist Jerome (347-420), contended that the apocrypha were not in the Old Testament because they were never received by the Jews as inspired

Scripture (see his Preface to the Books of Samuel and Kings).

Martin Luther, at his famous Leipzig debate with John Eck in 1519, first concluded that the Old Testament apocrypha were not inspired Scripture due to their dubious statements used to justify purgatory. The Reformers followed Luther and a long succession of early church fathers and medieval theologians. This debate prompted the Roman Catholic Council of Trent to define the limits of Scripture, the first ecumenical council to do so. In 1546 Trent affirmed that the Old Testament apocrypha were inspired Scripture. This was a striking conclusion given the many eminent Christian figures who believed the apocrypha were uninspired, which even included Luther's great theological nemesis, Cardinal Cajetan.

In light of Trent it was important the English Church produced an official position on the limits of Scripture. And Article 6 explicitly sides with Jerome ('as Hierome saith') in rejecting the apocrypha as inspired Scripture. The Bible was confined to the thirty-nine books of the Hebrew Old Testament and the twenty-seven New Testament books because their 'authority was never any doubt in the Church.' In other words, throughout the centuries as Christians have sought to discern which books are Spirit-inspired and which are not, there developed an unquestionable core. The apocrypha were too disputed to be included.

But Article 6 does not conclude that the apocrypha are useless. Rather, it affirms the books as helpful for an 'example of life and instruction of manners.' But the Article explains, the apocrypha cannot be used in the way inspired Scripture can: 'to establish any doctrine.' That is for the Bible alone.

The Significance of Scripture

Article 6's affirmation of the sufficiency and size of Scripture has immense significance for us today. Firstly, Scripture's sufficiency is currently a greatly neglected teaching. If Scripture is sufficient for the believer's conversion and conservation then Scripture must contain all we need for a healthy church life. Put another way, Scripture should provide the rationale for all church activity. However helpful management techniques and leadership methods may be, they do not in themselves contain the life-giving food that converts and conserves church members. Technique is only as useful as it helps promote the Christ clothed in Scripture.

Secondly, Scripture's sufficiency helps us grasp the place of popular disciplines like science and psychology. They may be useful in learning more about God's breathtaking world but they alone can never convert and conserve believers. Too often a discipline like psychology seeks to prescribe what is good or evil for humans. But psychology is unable to define what is good or evil. That is the prerogative of a purposeful creator alone. Psychology does well when it describes. It alone cannot prescribe. True, medical science may assist us to live more comfortably. But without Scripture this amounts to making the Titanic more luxurious as it sinks.

Disciplines like science and psychology are wonderful servants for a biblical worldview, but terrible masters. No matter how much we learn about the nature of sexual orientation (description), for example, it is for the one who designed sex to say how it is used (prescription).

Finally, the sufficiency and size of Scripture reminds us to derive our Christian beliefs from the sixty-six books of Scripture alone. No matter how old, attractive, or ornate, a church tradition is—if it cannot be established from Scripture, it cannot be imposed. On the other hand, the current postmodern climate pressures us to create and chose our own values: 'I have the right to believe what I like!' Not so in light of Scripture. If Christians are 'to establish doctrine' (about salvation) from Scripture's sixty-six books alone, then we have no choice but to test all beliefs against Scripture itself, no matter how culturally uncomfortable the conclusions may be.

The Revd Dr Martin Foord *is Senior Lecturer in Systematic Theology and Church History, and Dean of Ministry Development at Trinity Theological College, Perth, Australia.*

QUESTIONS FOR REFLECTION

1. Did the church give us the Bible, or vice-versa?
2. Does this Article mean that we should not read and study any other book except the Bible?
3. What status do you give to human traditions in your church?

PRAYER

Blessed Lord, who caused the unerring scriptures to be written for our learning: grant that we may hear, read, digest, and embrace them, and forever hold fast the joyful hope of life eternal, which they proclaim to us in Christ, in whose name we pray. *Amen.*

BIBLE READING

1 Corinthians 10:6-11

Now these things took place as examples for us, that we might not desire evil as they did. Do not be idolaters as some of them were; as it is written, 'The people sat down to eat and drink and rose up to play.' We must not indulge in sexual immorality as some of them did, and twenty-three thousand fell in a single day. We must not put Christ to the test, as some of them did and were destroyed by serpents, nor grumble, as some of them did and were destroyed by the Destroyer. Now these things happened to them as an example, but they were written down for our instruction, on whom the end of the ages has come.

STARTER QUESTION

In what ways is the Old Testament relevant for believers now that Christ has come?

ARTICLE VII

OF THE OLD TESTAMENT

The Old Testament is not contrary to
the New; for both in the Old and New
Testament everlasting life is offered to
mankind by Christ, who is the only
Mediator between God and man, being
both God and man. Wherefore there are not
to be heard which feign that the old fathers
did look only for transitory promises.
Although the law given from God by Moses,
as touching ceremonies and rites, do not
bind Christian men, nor the civil precepts
thereof ought of necessity to be received in
any commonwealth; yet, notwithstanding,
no Christian man whatsoever is free from
the obedience of the commandments which
are called moral.

ARTICLE VII

Article 6 has told us that the Bible is our sole authority for understanding the gospel of salvation, and listed the books of the Old and New Testaments. But then two questions immediately follow: (i) how does the Old Testament relate to the New? (ii) which Old Testament laws are binding on the New Testament believer? Article 7 answers both these questions, bringing together two separate Articles written by Thomas Cranmer in the 1550s.

RELATING THE OLD AND THE NEW

In the early Christian centuries, heretics like Marcion and the Gnostics threw away the Old Testament as redundant and unspiritual, and focused only on their favourite passages in the New. Many churches do the same today, often implicitly, by driving a wedge between the testaments and neglecting the Old. But Article 7 makes clear that they belong together and there is no contradiction between them. The Bible is one book, written by one God, and it teaches one overall message about salvation through faith in Jesus our Messiah and only Mediator. The Jewish Scriptures 'bear witness about me', says Jesus (John 5:39). Beginning with Moses and the prophets, he showed the disciples how the whole Old Testament points to himself (Luke 24:27).

Griffith Thomas puts it memorably in *The Principles of Theology*: the Old Testament is crowded with 'unfulfilled prophecies', 'unexplained ceremonies', and 'unsatisfied longings', all of which are met in Jesus Christ. From beginning to end—from Genesis 3:15 to Malachi 4:1—the Old Testament looks forward with anticipation to the arrival of the Messiah. Therefore, don't listen to those who claim that the patriarchs 'did look only for transitory promises.' On the contrary, God's people in the Old Testament recognised that the temporal blessings they enjoyed—like the Promised Land flowing with milk and honey—were only a foretaste of much better things to come. Abraham was a model believer, trusting the promises of God for eternal life. He lived as a nomad in a tent, but was 'looking forward to the city with foundations, whose architect and builder is God' (Hebrews 11:10). So keep reading and preaching the Old Testament, because it is full of the gospel of salvation through Jesus Christ.

APPLYING THE OLD TESTAMENT TODAY

The old and new covenants are not contradictory, but nor are they identical. There are continuities and discontinuities between them, especially in the application of Old Testament law. Article 7 divides the law into three types—ceremonial, civil, and moral. This explanation was popular among the Reformers, borrowed from medieval scholars like Thomas Aquinas, though it has been challenged by some recent Reformed theologians for imposing an external grid which would have surprised both Moses and Paul. Nevertheless, the threefold division remains a helpful shorthand and aide memoire.

The ceremonial law concerning priesthood and purity, sacrifice and sabbath, has all been fulfilled in Jesus Christ. These rituals were 'a shadow of the good things to come' (Colossians 2:17, Hebrews 10:1). Jesus is our great high priest and the ultimate sacrifice, so it is foolish to return to these old ceremonies which were merely signposts to the Saviour. There is no place in the Christian church for a special order of ordained priests, with their altars and ritual ablutions and eucharistic sacrifices. Such practices denigrate the glory and finality of the ministry of Jesus. Why return to the shadows when the reality is here?

The civil law concerning church-state relations and judicial punishments is also no longer binding on the Christian. The city of Münster, in northern Germany, stands as a famous warning to those who handle the Old Testament wrongly. In the 1530s, under the leadership of radical prophets, the city tried to reestablish a theocratic monarchy, modelled on the reigns of King David and King Solomon, including the reintroduction of polygamy. Many crimes were punishable by death (as laid down in the Mosaic law), such as blasphemy, adultery, and disrespect of parents. The Münster experiment ended in a bloodbath. Article 7 reminds us that those laws were intended only for the Old Testament nation of Israel, which had a specific purpose in God's salvation plan. Under the new covenant, Christian nations are free to develop their own constitutions and legal frameworks.

So what about the moral law, like the Ten Commandments? Opponents of the Reformers accused them of being Antinomians, because if we preach justification by faith alone not by works of the law (Romans 3:28, Galatians 2:16), won't that lead to lawlessness and immorality? If simply believing in Jesus is enough for salvation, why worry about moral behaviour? But in the Sermon on the Mount, Jesus tightens the moral law; he does not abolish it (Matthew 5:17-20). Both Old and New Testaments expound God's command, 'Be holy, as I am holy' (Leviticus 11:44, 1 Peter 1:16). So don't listen to those who pretend that provided we profess faith in Christ, it doesn't matter how we live. True Christian faith will always produce the fruit of holiness (see Article 12 for more on this).

THE HOLY SCRIPTURES AND THE HOLY SPIRIT

Cranmer's original Article on the Old Testament law ended with an extra warning (deleted by the Elizabethans): 'wherefore they are not to be hearkened unto, who affirm that Holy Scripture is given only to the weak, and do boast themselves continually of the Spirit, of whom (they say) they have learned such things as they teach, although the same be most evidently repugnant to the Holy Scripture.'

False teachers in every generation claim a special hot-line to the Holy Spirit as their reason for departing from the Bible. For example, the notorious German radical, Thomas Müntzer, asserted in his *Prague Manifesto* (1521) that we must listen to the direct voice of the Spirit, not to 'the dead letter of Scripture.' But God's Spirit never speaks in such a way as to contradict the Scriptures, because all Scripture is itself breathed out by God (2 Timothy 3:16). Sam Allberry tweeted, in the midst of recent controversy about God's will for the Church: '"Waiting for the Spirit to speak" about something sounds godly and humble. But if the Spirit has already spoken it's ungodly and arrogant' (@SamAllberry, 13 February 2017). That's classic Cranmerian theology compressed into 140 characters.

The Spirit and the Scriptures are always in harmony. The Old Testament and the New Testament always concur. So keep preaching the whole of the Bible—every part of it, from cover to cover—'the whole counsel of God' (Acts 20:27). Treasure, study, and obey the whole of God's written Word, because it is the excellent and urgent message of salvation to a needy world.

The Revd Dr Andrew Atherstone *is Tutor in History and Doctrine at Wycliffe Hall in Oxford.*

Questions for reflection

1. Do you read or preach from the Old Testament as much as you do from the New Testament?
2. What are the potential pitfalls when we are thinking about the application of the Old Testament to today?
3. Should Christian churches imitate the Old Testament temple style of worship?

Prayer

Everlasting and unchangeable God: grant us the faith
of our father Abraham that we may grasp hold of all
you have promised and obey all you have commanded,
for the sake of your Son, Jesus Christ, our only
mediator and Lord. *Amen.*

BIBLE READING
1 Corinthians 15:3-7

For I delivered to you as of first importance what I also received: that Christ died for our sins in accordance with the Scriptures, that he was buried, that he was raised on the third day in accordance with the Scriptures, and that he appeared to Cephas, then to the twelve. Then he appeared to more than five hundred brothers at one time, most of whom are still alive, though some have fallen asleep. Then he appeared to James, then to all the apostles.

STARTER QUESTION

Why does the apostle Paul stress these particular things of 'first importance'?

ARTICLE VIII

OF THE THREE CREEDS

~

The Three creeds, Nicene Creed,
Athanasius's Creed, and that which is
commonly called the Apostles' Creed, ought
thoroughly to be received and believed:
for they may be proved by most certain
warrants of holy Scripture.

ARTICLE VIII

S ome of the Thirty-nine Articles were particularly contentious and reflective of the controversies of the sixteenth-century Reformation in England and the Continent. Not so Article 8.

Article 8 is a central statement around which Christians have agreed, namely advocating assent to the three central creeds as touchstones of authentic Christian faith. This is hardly to suggest that there are no contentious issues or causes of debate in the early centuries of the Church (briefly touched on below). However, it was universally agreed across the Eastern and Western Church that these creeds summarise the core belief of the universal Church. Hence, as the Article commends, they 'ought thoroughly to be received and believed', not least because their content may be found in Scripture.

However, despite widespread assent to these three creeds in the sixteenth and seventeenth century, the same is not true today. In the twenty-first century there is contention over the function—and sometimes the theology—of the three creeds. Why? For three reasons, in ascending seriousness:

First, the creeds are not consistently recited in Anglican public worship. Maybe some believe them to be too formulaic, or jarring with an age which sees little pedagogical value in rote repetition.

Secondly, as a consequence of the previous point perhaps, the creeds—particularly, but not exclusively, the Athanasian Creed—

are unknown to today's Anglicans. Hence, far from being a touchstone of orthodoxy, they do not provide the true test of authentic faith as they were intended to.

Thirdly, also as a consequence of the above, the creeds often are ignored when matters of public discourse and debate surface. The Church of England is in danger of forgetting the lessons learnt by previous generations which led to the formation of the creeds. Equally disappearing from view are the Thirty-nine Articles themselves, the *Book of Common Prayer*, and the Canons of the Church.

BRIEF OVERVIEW OF CONTENT OF THE THREE CREEDS

The Apostles' Creed succinctly summarises the core belief in God the Father, God the Son, and God the Holy Spirit, which is necessary for salvation:

God the Father is creator of all in heaven and earth. God the Son is conceived by the Holy Spirit, incarnated in human flesh, crucified, died, rose, and ascended into heaven with the Father, and will come again as judge. God the Holy Spirit, through whom we are made members of the universal church, helps us know the forgiveness of sins and eternal life.

The Nicene Creed contains the same Trinitarian formula of belief in one God, who is Father and creator of all; the only, and eternally begotten Son, of the same substance with the Father; and the life-giving Holy Spirit. This creed expands the core beliefs, to speak of the entirety of the creation as of the Father, the very essence and being of the Son as being the same as the Father, and the Holy Spirit's 'procession', or 'double procession' from the Father and the Son (the *Filioque* clause). In addition, following on from the historic Council of Nicaea, here is a confident affirmation of the holy, catholic (universal), and apostolic Church, for which baptism is essential for forgiveness and true membership.

The Athanasian Creed begins very differently: 'whosoever wishes to be saved...must hold the catholic faith... (which is) this...'

The three triads 'such as the Father is, such as the Son is, such as the Holy Spirit is...' emphasise the equality and divinity of all three persons of the Trinity. Moreover, whilst we are to confess faith in each person of the Trinity, we are in no way to infer that there are three Gods. Nor should we assume that by so emphasising the co-equal divinity of all three persons that we thereby deny the incarnation and humanity of our Lord Jesus Christ.

ARTICLE 8 FOR TODAY

According to the *Book of Common Prayer*, the Apostles' Creed is meant to be recited at Morning and Evening Prayer, and the Nicene Creed is part of the service of Holy Communion. Athanasius's Creed is prescribed instead of the Apostles' Creed on fourteen occasions during the liturgical year (including Christmas Day, Easter Day, Ascension Day, Pentecost, and Trinity Sunday). *Common Worship* contains a shortened, responsive version of the Athanasian Creed for those who cannot quite make it through the strong meat of the full edition.

It seems to me that ensuring the three creeds are used in our corporate worship is highly desirable! Here are four Anglican reasons why I believe this to be the case:

1. Our faith is public: Neither in the Scriptures nor in our liturgy, is faith thought of as merely a private, personal affair. 'Let the word of God dwell among you (*plural*), it says in Colossians 3:16. Yes, it must be private and personal, but it must also be public and corporate. Along with the sacraments of Baptism and the Lord's Supper, Anglican liturgy assumes that our worship is a public declaration.

2. Our faith requires active assent: We are called to believe with our heart, and confess with our lips, in order to be saved (see Romans 10:9-10). The act of consenting to the biblical beliefs of the Church is necessary for salvation. This is more than recitation of the creeds, but surely not less?

3. Our faith is corporate and communal: In an individualistic age we want to affirm that corporate worship, somehow, and in God's providence, is more than the sum of the individuals' present. Whatever we believe about prophecy in this context, the same principle should work with our public declarations: 'if an unbeliever or an inquirer comes in while everyone is prophesying, they are convicted of sin and are brought under judgment by all… exclaiming, 'God is really among you!'" (1 Corinthians 14:24-25).

4. Our faith is liturgical: It may well be that early forms of the creeds lie behind 1 Corinthians 15:3-7, Philippians 2:5-11, and 2 Timothy 2:8-13. If this is the case then we have the earliest commendation of a form of set liturgy, to be recited in public worship. The *Book of Common Prayer* gives us a pattern of worship which has stood the test of time, and when replaced by less formal (or no) liturgies is invariably weaker.

So, in the light of Article 8, let us publicly, believingly, actively, corporately, communally, and liturgically affirm our belief in the triune God!

The Revd Dr Simon Vibert *is the Vicar of Christ Church, Virginia Water and author of several books, including The Perpetual Battle: the World, the Flesh, and the Devil (Christian Focus, 2018)*

QUESTIONS FOR REFLECTION

1. Should we use the Creeds in public worship, or save them for private instruction?
2. What things of first importance would you include in a creed today?
3. What gives the creeds their authority, according to the Article?

PRAYER

Almighty God, who enables us to follow the pattern of life-giving doctrine which was once for all delivered to the saints: by the help of your Holy Spirit, strengthen us to guard the good deposit of the faith, for the glory of our Saviour, Jesus Christ. *Amen.*

BIBLE READING

Psalm 51:1-6

Have mercy on me, O God,
    according to your steadfast love;
  according to your abundant mercy
      blot out my transgressions.
Wash me thoroughly from my iniquity,
    and cleanse me from my sin!
For I know my transgressions,
    and my sin is ever before me.
Against you, you only, have I sinned
    and done what is evil in your sight,
so that you may be justified in your words
    and blameless in your judgment.
Behold, I was brought forth in iniquity,
    and in sin did my mother conceive me.
Behold, you delight in truth in the inward being,
    and you teach me wisdom in the secret heart.

STARTER QUESTION

What is sin, and how deep does it go?

ARTICLE IX

OF ORIGINAL OR BIRTH-SIN

~

Original Sin standeth not in the following of Adam, (as the Pelagians do vainly talk), but it is the fault and corruption of the Nature of every man, that naturally is ingendered of the offspring of Adam; whereby man is very far gone from original righteousness, and is of his own nature inclined to evil, so that the flesh lusteth [*concupiscat*] always contrary to the spirit; and therefore in every person born into this world, it deserveth God's wrath and damnation. And this infection of nature doth remain, yea in them that are regenerated; whereby the lust of the flesh, called in the Greek, '*Phronema Sarkos*', which some do expound the wisdom, some sensuality, some the affection, some the desire, of the flesh, is not subject to the Law of God. And although there is no condemnation for them that believe and are baptized, yet the Apostle doth confess, that concupiscence and lust hath of itself the nature of sin.

ARTICLE IX

Having laid down the foundations of who God is and how we come to think rightly about him (through Scripture as interpreted by the creeds), we now arrive at the beginning of God's work of salvation for humanity. Before turning to the good news, we must hear the bad news, the black backdrop against which the jewel of the gospel can shine most brightly.

Article 9, 'Of Original or Birth Sin,' shows us just how bad we really are. Amongst the various technical terms is an utterly shocking analysis of human nature. Contemporary debates within the Church of England, as well as society more widely, desperately need to hear this biblical anthropology.

THE SOURCE OF ORIGINAL SIN
First, let us see the source of original sin. It's not just about our environment (copying the bad examples around us, tracing their way back to Adam) affecting a neutral human nature. The fifth-century bishop, Augustine, standing in a long line of African leaders who have had to speak out against British false teaching, corrected Pelagius on just this point. Drawing on texts such as Psalm 51:5 ('Surely I was sinful at birth, sinful from the time my mother conceived me'), he argued that our very nature is corrupted. Every single person born in Adam's race is 'inclined to evil.'

Yes, we are made in God's image (Genesis 1:26–27), but our

nature is now positively faulty at the deepest level as a result of the fall. This means that just because we desire something, or find pleasure in something, does not make it good. We are not as we should be. Our 'natural' desires must be evaluated in light of God's word.

THE CONSEQUENCES OF ORIGINAL SIN

Secondly, let us consider the consequences of original sin. Our nature is sinful and it therefore deserves 'God's wrath and damnation.' The problem with humanity is not just that we make life miserable for each other, but that we face the justice and holiness of our perfect creator God. When he assesses our nature—whether we are male or female, in utero or in a care home, straight or gay, Northern or Southern, or whatever other divisions we might imagine—he judges that it is 'very far gone from original righteousness' and so we all deserve to face the consequences.

The Bible tells us that 'the wages of sin is death' (Romans 6:23), that ultimate and fearful experience of God's wrath. This is why all of humanity so desperately needs to receive Jesus as Lord and Saviour. It is easy to lose this eternal perspective and become engrossed in the here-and-now, so may the dire consequences of original sin fire our passion for sharing the gospel whenever we can.

THE PERSISTENCE OF ORIGINAL SIN

Thirdly, let us acknowledge the persistence of original sin. When anyone is born again by the Holy Spirit, coming to Christ in repentance and faith, receiving the sacrament of baptism, there is then 'no condemnation' (Romans 8:1). Nevertheless, the sinful human nature remains, persistently waging war against the work of God's indwelling Holy Spirit (Romans 8:5–13). Our sinful desires ('concupiscence', often used to translate the Greek *epithumia*) still bubble away inside.

Were it not for the justifying work of Christ and the continual sanctifying work of the Spirit, we would be no different to anyone else. Indeed, this is why we pray daily: 'Almighty and most merciful Father… there is no health in us: But thou, O Lord, have mercy upon us miserable offenders…' As Anglicans we are realistic about who we are, even as believers—people who are continually dependent on God's mercy, even after conversion, and people who are engaged in a lifelong battle between our sinful human nature and God's indwelling Spirit (Galatians 5:16–25 and Romans 6–7). Just as the tenth commandment shows us that even our desires must be subjected to God's will, so now as believers we must fight against all fleshly desires which are hostile to God and his good will for his creation.

Historically, the ninth Article was written to combat errors propagated by the Roman Catholic church, particularly the Council of Trent, which tended to downplay just how bad we are as a result of the fall. So too today there will be those whose theology lacks serious engagement with the reality of our fallen nature. This might be articulate theologians arguing for the blessing of human desire in various unbiblical forms. Or it might be a 'normal' Christian, who doesn't see a problem with doing what feels good to them as long as no one really gets hurt. Both need to return to God's analysis of human nature and realise the profound corruption that lies at the heart of human experience and desire.

Article 9 is vital to healthy, biblical Christianity, for 'superficiality in our consciousness of the nature and power of sin will tend not merely to a superficial statement of the Atonement of Christ, but to the destruction of the idea of atonement itself' (Griffith Thomas). Before long we will reach those Articles that speak of the wonderful saving work of Christ, but for now let us return in contrition to our merciful God and Father, 'from whom all holy desires … do proceed.'

The Revd John Percival *is a PhD candidate at the University of Cambridge and the Production Editor of Churchman.*

QUESTIONS FOR REFLECTION

1. Are unholy thoughts and desires only displeasing to God if we act on them?
2. In what ways do we downplay or ignore the reality and depths of sin in our hearts?
3. How might we wrongly 'accumulate teachers to suit our own sinful passions' (2 Timothy 4:3)?

PRAYER

Lord God, because without you we are not able to please you: mercifully grant us repentance and a knowledge of your truth, that we may turn from our manifold sins and wickedness and be saved, through Jesus Christ our sinless saviour. *Amen.*

BIBLE READING

Romans 8:1-8

There is therefore now no condemnation for those who are in Christ Jesus. For the law of the Spirit of life has set you free in Christ Jesus from the law of sin and death. For God has done what the law, weakened by the flesh, could not do. By sending his own Son in the likeness of sinful flesh and for sin, he condemned sin in the flesh, in order that the righteous requirement of the law might be fulfilled in us, who walk not according to the flesh but according to the Spirit. For those who live according to the flesh set their minds on the things of the flesh, but those who live according to the Spirit set their minds on the things of the Spirit. For to set the mind on the flesh is death, but to set the mind on the Spirit is life and peace. For the mind that is set on the flesh is hostile to God, for it does not submit to God's law; indeed, it cannot. Those who are in the flesh cannot please God.

STARTER QUESTION

Can people who are not born again do anything to please God?

ARTICLE X

OF FREE WILL

~

The condition of Man after the fall of Adam
is such, that he cannot turn and prepare
himself, by his own natural strength and
good works, to faith, and calling upon
God: Wherefore we have no power to do
good works pleasant and acceptable to
God, without the grace of God by Christ
preventing us, that we may have a good will,
and working with us, when we have that
good will.

ARTICLE X

A rticle 10 claims to be about *free* will, but might more clearly be titled, 'Of the *bondage* of the will.' The Article does not stress the freedom and ability of the natural human will, but its slavery and inability: 'the condition of man after the fall of Adam is such, that he *cannot...*'

The bondage and inability of the natural human will was one of the earliest theological principles of the Protestant Reformation. In 1525, Martin Luther penned *On the Bondage of the Will* to rebut the humanist Catholic scholar Desiderius Erasmus, whose *On Free Will* had been published a year earlier. The Latin title of our Article may be identical to Erasmus's title, but its theology (rooted in Augustine's teaching) is identical to Luther's!

GRACE AND SALVATION

Why was the bondage of the will so central to Reformation theology? It is because it is part-and-parcel of the nature of God's grace and our salvation.

The unreformed Roman church did not consider itself Pelagian: it taught the absolute necessity of God's grace for salvation. But in the theology of the dominant 'Modern Way' (*via moderna*)—which was officially sanctioned as dogma at the Council of Trent—grace worked in a particular way. In short, a man or woman had to do their best to believe, seek, love, and obey God; if they did so, God would treat their paltry efforts as *if* it were perfect righteousness. This was summed up in the medieval axiom, 'God will not deny grace to the one who does their best'—or, colloquially, 'Do your best: God does the rest.'

Fundamental to the *via moderna* model was the principle that human beings had at least *some* natural ability within themselves to turn to God in penitence and faith—*some* innate capacity to do good works. In particular, the doctrine demanded that the human will had to be sufficiently free and able to respond to the offer of God's grace. The Council of Trent accordingly expressly anathematised those who taught that 'the free will of man is lost and extinguished.' On this matter, the post-Reformation Roman church has been remarkably consistent. The *Catechism of the Catholic Church* (1994) is as emphatic as Trent was that man's nature is such that 'he might of his own accord seek his Creator' (paragraph 1730).

Article 10's explicit denial of a man's ability to 'turn and prepare himself' for faith is thus a direct repudiation of a fundamental presupposition of the Roman doctrine, and a vital step in the evangelical understanding of the gospel. It is the logical outworking of Article 9 with respect to humanity's natural standing before God, and the logical prerequisite for Article 11's teaching on how believers are justified by God in Christ by faith alone. Only with belief in Article 10's account of our inveterate disinclination and utter inability in ourselves to call upon God, can we have a gospel of salvation that is truly by grace *alone*.

Article 10, ostensibly about human will, is thus in reality fundamentally about securing the sheer graciousness of divine grace in the economy of salvation. Given Article 10, I have nothing to boast in except Christ crucified.

IMPLICATIONS FOR US TODAY

Polemically, Article 10 reminds us of an enduring fundamental difference between us and Rome. In this 500th anniversary of the Reformation it is fashionable both to express regret about the division in the church, and to claim that most of the differences were exaggerated and have now been overcome. Article 10 emphatically declares 'Not so!'

Article 10 underwrites a *monergistic* doctrine of justification (from *mono*—'one,' and *ergo*—'to work'). This contrasts it with a *synergistic* doctrine ('*syn*'—together; so 'working together'). It teaches that our state of spiritual death—the utter inability of the bound human will—means that everything that goes into our coming to spiritual life has to belong to God. His is the whole initiative; his is the decisive, effective will.

The Roman church still baulks at Article 10, because it still teaches synergism—the cooperation of a man or woman with God for salvation. Admittedly, since Article 10 was written, Protestant versions of synergism have arisen—even within the Anglican fold (Arminianism, Wesleyanism)—with the effect of obscuring what was once a clear dividing-line between Rome and the churches of the Reformation. But at root there is still no compromise possible nor middle ground conceivable between monergism and synergism: either the work is God's alone, or it is not. Article 10 continues to put doctrinal distance between us and Rome.

Apologetically, Article 10 should make us careful about how we talk about 'free will' in our defence of the Christian faith. We can and should talk about free will—even if we are impeccable Calvinists!—as part of our apologetic, provided we do so in a manner consonant with Articles 9 and 10. Why is there so much evil in our world? Men and women freely will it. For what are unbelievers judged and punished by a just and holy God? For what they have freely willed and done. When we sin, we sin freely and willingly. No-one else forces us to choose evil—not the Devil, not even Adam; and above all, not God. Our wills are by nature free, but free to will only as our nature directs: that is, to sin.

But 'free will' must *not* feature in our answers to questions about faith and salvation. In answering the questions, 'Why do you believe?' or 'Why are you saved?', we must not reach *within*— to our 'free will,' our 'natural strength and good works'—to answer. Article 10 forbids it, because Scripture forbids it (Ephesians 2:1-10). We must reach entirely outside ourselves, to the merit of Christ and the grace of God.

Personally, Article 10 should instil in us the great gospel-wrought virtues of hope, humility, and gratitude:

1. Hope: Article 10 is not, despite its bleak view of the human will, a counsel of despair but a counsel of hope. If in the gospel, life is promised to me—despite knowing that I am *dead* in my sins and transgressions—then that promise cannot but offer real, un-quenchable hope; *especially* to those who know more clearly than others the sinfulness of their hearts.

2. Humility: If it weren't for Article 10, I could still find things to boast in—not least that I, unlike those deplorable unbelievers, have freely chosen to seek after God! Belief in the *ability* of human will freely to turn to God for salvation, if it isn't swallowed by the Charybdis of despair, will sooner or later be shipwrecked on the Scylla of pride.

3. Gratitude: What an amazing, generous God we have who loves those described in Article 10! He loves those who, left alone, would not love him. When I see what I am like (Articles 9 and 10), I marvel at what God is like. And I know the only appropriate response is a life of humble thankfulness.

The Revd Dr Tom Woolford *is the Curate of All Hallows, Bispham in the Diocese of Blackburn.*

QUESTIONS FOR REFLECTION

1. In what ways does being a Christian transform how we think and act?
2. Can someone be argued or forced into becoming a Christian?
3. Why is prayer such a vital part of the Christian life and evangelism?

PRAYER

Lord God, the strength of all who put their trust in you:
because through the weakness of our human nature we
cannot do anything good without you, grant us the help
of your grace both to will and to work for your good
pleasure, through Jesus Christ our hope. *Amen.*

BIBLE READING

Romans 3:21-26

But now the righteousness of God has been manifested apart from the law, although the Law and the Prophets bear witness to it—the righteousness of God through faith in Jesus Christ for all who believe. For there is no distinction: for all have sinned and fall short of the glory of God, and are justified by his grace as a gift, through the redemption that is in Christ Jesus, whom God put forward as a propitiation by his blood, to be received by faith. This was to show God's righteousness, because in his divine forbearance he had passed over former sins. It was to show his righteousness at the present time, so that he might be just and the justifier of the one who has faith in Jesus.

STARTER QUESTION

How can God be right when he says we are righteous, when we're clearly not?

ARTICLE XI

OF THE JUSTIFICATION OF MAN

~

We are accounted righteous before God, only for the merit of our Lord and Saviour Jesus Christ by Faith, and not for our own works or deservings: Wherefore, that we are justified by Faith only is a most wholesome Doctrine, and very full of comfort, as more largely is expressed in the Homily of Justification.

ARTICLE XI

Allof the Protestant churches, at the point where they split from Rome, produced doctrinal standards to explain why they were no longer part of a unified Western church. The Thirty-nine Articles arose out of a desire to explain both the commitments of the Church of England, and the errors of Rome. After ten Articles on the nature of God, Scripture, and the predicament of man, Article 11 takes us to the heart of Reformation doctrine. The same priority is seen in the homilies, where the Homily on Justification comes third.

For Cranmer, and the Anglican Reformers this is a critical doctrine. Indeed, the homily states plainly, 'this is the strong Rock and foundation of Christian Religion', so much so that 'whosoever denieth, is not to be accounted for a Christian man'. This is a primary doctrine; to deny it is to not be a Christian at all. Yet the Article is at pains to stress that it is a doctrine *very full of comfort*.

ROMAN CATHOLIC DOCTRINE

The Church of Rome taught (e.g. Council of Trent, Session 6 Chapter 5) that the grace of God, earned by Jesus, is infused into the soul of the believer. The believer then co-operates with God in living a holy life and thus, on the final day, the believer will be justified by God on the basis of the good works achieved in co-operation with grace. Rome taught, in other words, that the basis of justification is the life of the believer, which will be good enough if grace has been received and the believer has worked hard enough.

This doctrine is offensive to the gospel, for Paul says that all works have to be excluded from justification 'so that no one can boast' (Ephesians 2:9). It robs Christ of the glory which is his. As the Article says, 'We are accounted righteous before God, only for the merit of our Lord and Saviour Jesus Christ by Faith, and not of our own works or deservings.'

Article 11 directs us to the Homily on Justification, where Cranmer makes clear in the first place that every man is guilty of sin before God, so that 'every man of necessity is constrained to seek for another righteousness.' God is perfect, and he demands perfect obedience from us. Since we cannot obey God, we are rightly under condemnation. Justification brings us into the courtroom of God, and we are guilty as charged. But what we are incapable of doing, Christ did for us.

CHRIST'S WORK AND OURS

What has Christ accomplished for us? First, he came 'to fulfil the Law for us'. When we put our faith in Christ, we are brought into such a relationship with Christ that Martin Luther calls it a marriage. Christ's righteous life becomes ours, and our sin becomes his. We do not, therefore, come to stand before God, offering our imperfect lives to him and trusting that this will be good enough. Instead, we stand before God with the perfect life of Christ credited to our account, so that God can justly say that we are righteous in his sight.

Secondly, Christ then, 'by the shedding of his most precious blood' made 'a sacrifice and satisfaction'. The guilt of sin needed to receive the punishment of death. Christ, standing in our place, took the full anger of God at all our sin and paid the full penalty for sin. Cranmer therefore affirms Paul's statement that 'No man is justified by works of the Law' for it is 'only for the merit of our Lord and Saviour Jesus Christ.'

This doctrine preserves the honour of Christ as the only Saviour, but it also magnifies God's justice. If God accepted our incomplete obedience as the ground of our justification, it would demonstrate that his standards are less than perfect, and so would undo the very nature of God. But the work of Christ proves that God is both perfectly righteous, and full of mercy, as Romans 3:26 teaches. God is able today to declare righteous those who will stand before his judgment seat clothed in the righteousness of Christ.

What, then, must the Christian do? The Homily is very careful at this point. On the one hand, it affirms that a truly justified person will not then be idle; rather, we will 'render ourselves unto God wholly with all our will, hearts, might and power, and serve him in all good deeds, obeying his commandments during our lives.' Yet, on the other hand, Cranmer will not allow us to think that our good works play any part in our justification: 'we must renounce the merit of all our said virtues.' Our deeds may indeed be good, but they are never good *enough*. Justification 'is not a thing which we render unto him, but which we receive of him.' Even faith is not a good work, but only the means by which we claim the promises of Christ.

COMFORTING DOCTRINE

How, then, is this doctrine 'very full of comfort'? It is in this: that the believer can have total assurance of salvation before God. The Roman Catholic, whose judgment is in the future, and whose case rests on their good deeds, can never have assurance of salvation. Have I done enough good? What if I do something bad tomorrow that tips the scales against me? The committed Catholic will be full of anxiety, as indeed Luther was before his conversion.

But we know that justification is not by works, but purely by the merits of Christ. We do not look to our own deeds, but the perfect and completed work of Christ, imputed to our account. Our position is so certain that the future judgment has been declared now—and in declaring it so, God has made it so: 'You are my children'; we are new creations (2 Corinthians 5:17-21). Yes, we will continue to sin. But we confront our sinfulness, bring it to the cross, repent and walk away free men and women, justified freely by faith alone.

The Revd Ash Carter *is Curate of Westminster at One, a PhD candidate at the University of Leicester, and Hon. Treasurer of Church Society.*

QUESTIONS FOR REFLECTION

1. How does this Article relate to the previous 2?
2. Why is the doctrine of justification by faith alone so 'very full of comfort'?
3. How central is this doctrine to your life and that of your church?

PRAYER

Merciful Father, judge of all people and redeemer of
those who put their faith in you: fill our hearts with
gratitude and joy for the robes of righteousness in
which you clothe us, through the merits of our Lord
and Saviour Jesus Christ. *Amen.*

BIBLE READING

Luke 6:43-49

For no good tree bears bad fruit, nor again does a bad tree bear good fruit, for each tree is known by its own fruit. For figs are not gathered from thornbushes, nor are grapes picked from a bramble bush. The good person out of the good treasure of his heart produces good, and the evil person out of his evil treasure produces evil, for out of the abundance of the heart his mouth speaks. Why do you call me 'Lord, Lord,' and not do what I tell you? Everyone who comes to me and hears my words and does them, I will show you what he is like: he is like a man building a house, who dug deep and laid the foundation on the rock. And when a flood arose, the stream broke against that house and could not shake it, because it had been well built. But the one who hears and does not do them is like a man who built a house on the ground without a foundation. When the stream broke against it, immediately it fell, and the ruin of that house was great.

STARTER QUESTION

How can you tell if someone is angry, or if they are happy, since emotions as such are invisible?

ARTICLE XII

OF GOOD WORKS

~

Albeit that Good Works, which are the
fruits of Faith, and follow after Justification,
cannot put away our sins, and endure the
severity of God's Judgement; yet are they
pleasing and acceptable to God in Christ,
and do spring out necessarily of a true and
lively Faith; insomuch that by them a lively
Faith may be as evidently known as a tree
discerned by the fruit.

ARTICLE XII

We proceed in the Christian life the same way that we began, in dependence upon the gospel word of God (1 Peter 1:23–25). God's word is our foundation and it is God's word that ensures the building built upon that foundation (i.e. our lives and ministries) is strong and straight (Colossians 2:6–7).

Throughout Scripture we hear the call to (i) listen to God's word; and (ii) do God's word, letting this word shape our thinking, emotions, and actions; and (iii) guard God's word (Matthew 7:24–27; James 1:22; 1 Timothy 6:20). The second of these, 'do God's word', is the subject of Article 12.

THE FRUIT OF FAITH

One of the charges levelled at the Reformation was that its teaching about grace and justification left no motivation for good works. Martin Luther famously answered this charge by saying, 'Our faith in Christ does not free us from works but from false opinions concerning works, that is, from the foolish presumption that justification is acquired by works' (*The Freedom of a Christian*, 1520). He later wrote, 'O it is a living, busy, active, mighty thing, this faith. It is impossible for it not to be doing good works incessantly. It does not ask whether good works are to be done, but before the question is asked, it has already done them, and is constantly doing them' (*Preface to Romans*, 1522).

Good works are the fruit of faith. They cannot justify us before God. They flow out of our justification, a result of God's Spirit working within us. As the Spirit brings God's word to our hearts, it shapes our thinking, emotions, and actions, leading to a life that is characterised by obedience and good works. These good works are a sign that we are no longer living for ourselves, but, rather, we are now living to glorify God. This results in a life pleasing to him, as we love and serve others. Luther again: we 'live in Christ through faith and in our neighbour through love' (*The Freedom of a Christian*).

Through the centuries, Christians have found it difficult to keep the cross central and dominant in our lives and thoughts. When our focus is off the cross, the only other option is that our focus is more on ourselves.

Two particular dangers need to be avoided. Firstly, we can fall into the trap of minimising grace and imagining that Jesus' death was not enough to deal with our sin. We can deceive ourselves that his cross was not enough to remove my particular guilt and shame. Or we can despair that someone else we know could ever be forgiven.

The other danger comes from the opposite direction. We can minimise our sin, and imagine our good works can somehow contribute to our salvation. Here in particular, Article 12 comes to our aid. It reminds us that good works flow from being justified. There is nothing inside us that is capable of choosing to do good. Even our best is not good enough. That is why we need God to work within us (Psalm 53; Romans 3:21-31).

SIGNS OF LIFE
So Article 12 is a great antidote to pride while at the same time an encouragement to godliness and good works, not as a payment or

contribution to my salvation but as the fruits of faith. Doing good works does not save me. I do good works because I am saved.

Article 12 also serves as a warning. If we confess to being a Christian and yet have no good works, we are like a tree with no fruit. And a tree that bears no fruit, has ceased to be a tree. In fact, it has stopped growing. It is no longer alive. It is dead (James 2:14-26).

So this Article is also an enormous encouragement. My good works are the result of God working in me. Good works are a sign of life, a testimony that my relationship with God is real and makes a difference to my life. In others, good works are the fruit by which they are known (Matthew 7:16-20). It's a great comfort to know God has planned the good works in which he wants me to walk because they then remind me why I was created and the purpose for which I was redeemed (Ephesians 2:8-10). Our lives are not random and meaningless. At every point there is a good work for us to walk in.

We can be encouraged by the word of God in which God addresses each one of us:

'For the grace of God has appeared that offers salvation to all people. It teaches us to say 'No' to ungodliness and worldly passions, and to live self-controlled, upright and godly lives in this present age, while we wait for the blessed hope—the appearing of the glory of our great God and Saviour, Jesus Christ, who gave himself for us to redeem us from all wickedness and to purify for himself a people that are his very own, eager to do what is good.' (Titus 2:11–14)

Jane Tooher *is Director of the Priscilla and Aquila Centre, and Lectures in Ministry, New Testament, Church History at Moore Theological College in Sydney, Australia.*

QUESTIONS FOR REFLECTION

1. What would you say to someone who said they were a Christian, but their life declared otherwise?
2. Are good works essential to salvation?
3. How can you guard against falling into legalism in the Christian life?

PRAYER

Almighty God, whose grace teaches us to say no to ungodliness and worldly passions: change our hearts that we may live self-controlled, upright, and godly lives as we wait for the return of our glorious Lord and spotless Saviour, Jesus Christ, in whose precious name we pray.
Amen.

BIBLE READING

Ephesians 2:1-5

And you were dead in the trespasses and sins in which you once walked, following the course of this world, following the prince of the power of the air, the spirit that is now at work in the sons of disobedience—among whom we all once lived in the passions of our flesh, carrying out the desires of the body and the mind, and were by nature children of wrath, like the rest of mankind. But God, being rich in mercy, because of the great love with which he loved us, even when we were dead in our trespasses, made us alive together with Christ— by grace you have been saved.

STARTER QUESTION

What can dead people do?

ARTICLE XIII

OF WORKS BEFORE JUSTIFICATION

~

Works done before the grace of Christ, and the Inspiration of his Spirit, are not pleasant to God, forasmuch as they spring not of faith in Jesus Christ, neither do they make men meet to receive grace, or (as the School-authors say) deserve grace of congruity: yea rather, for that they are not done as God hath willed and commanded them to be done, we doubt not but they have the nature of sin.

Article XIII

Article 13 is one of the three consecutive Articles that set out human works in their relation to salvation in Christ. Article 12 deals with the significance of the good works of believing Christians. Article 13 condemns a way of thinking about human status and capability before God. And Article 14 discusses 'works of supererogation' (see the next chapter to find out what *they* are!).

Of the three, Article 13 may seem strange to us today. But it is, in fact, one of the top five most referenced Articles of the Thirty-nine Articles. The teaching refuted in Article 13 is everywhere! You hear it when Frank Sinatra sings, *My Way*. You read it in Charles Dickens' short story *A Christmas Carol*, or watch it unfold in Frank Capra's film *It's a Wonderful Life*. You hear it referenced when a person confronted with the gospel choice says, 'But I am a good enough person, and God is a God of love. I am sure he will accept me.' It is referenced in the brief eulogies we've all heard at the crematorium. The vicar talks more of *how good* the deceased person was, to trail off vaguely into how they are 'in God's love now.' Leaving the listener to make the connections of the 'how' between the two. Conclusion: the gospel is about being good, and that being good makes you fit for heaven.

To understand what Article 13 means for us we need to start with what it meant at the time it was written. Article 13 rejects a form of preparation for conversion. It was a concept of preparation that sprang from the nominalist school of theologians ('as the School-authors say'). So let's go back a bit.

MEDIEVAL ERRORS

The medieval nominalists believed that God's natural gifts of reason and conscience had not been destroyed in us by the Fall. Were there not countless examples of unbelievers who loved neighbour above the self? And what of Scriptures like Luke 11:9, 'If you seek me, you will find me,' or James 4:8, 'Draw near to God, and he will draw near to you'?

With such concerns in mind, they reasoned that there was a prior step to salvation. They thought that if God rewards good works done in a state of infused grace, with eternal life as its just reward—could he not also reward good works done in a state of nature with an infusion of grace? The nominalist answer was, 'Yes.' The man or woman who does his or her best in a state of nature receives grace as a fitting reward (as the Article says, they 'deserve grace of congruity').

Nominalists were convinced that God meant for people to acquire grace first as a 'semi-merit' within a state of nature *by doing their best with their natural abilities.* And if that person did their best with those abilities, God would then grant them infused grace to earn salvation. This theology taught that people could *initiate* their salvation.

The Reformers rightly rejected the nominalist notion of grace by semi-merit within a state of nature. They called nominalists the 'new Pelagians.' They insisted that God's word says humanity is totally unable to move toward God, teaching that salvation is by his grace alone (Romans 3:21-26). They understood that humanity by its very nature was dead in its trespasses and sins (Ephesians 2:1-3) and that *all* our righteous deeds are like a polluted garment (Isaiah 64:6) before him.

As Article 13 asserts, even the seemingly good works of those who have not yet come to a saving faith are actually accounted by God as 'sin' and 'unpleasant' (Romans 8:8 and Hebrews 11:6). There is nothing an unregenerate person can do to make God smile! Yet it is unlikely that many ordinary Christians would accept this teaching at all, and some would find it very surprising or disturbing.

Yet Article 13 warns us that 'grace of congruity' turns the gospel on its head. It diminishes, if not destroys, the mercy and grace of God. Instead of turning us toward Christ and the blessings that are ours in him, we are turned inward to ourselves. It underlines the default position of every fallen human heart.

Startled by Godly Fear

Do you know what is the very first mark of grace in your life? It is when you start to wonder if what the Bible says may be true. And if it is true, that it may have uncovered a deep need in you that at times you sense and at times you hide. Rosaria Butterfield describes it in *Secret Thoughts of an Unlikely Convert*. When confronted by a friend who noticed that all her reading of the Bible was changing her, she said, 'What would you say if I told you that I'm beginning to believe that Jesus is real, is real and risen and loving and judging Lord, and that I am in big trouble?'

When God calls us into a saving knowledge of the Lord Jesus Christ, he must startle us with godly fear, a fear that alerts us to our lack and our need of God's goodness and grace (2 Corinthians 7:10). It dawns on us that there is a gap between his holiness and our sinfulness that we cannot breach. The more I know of him and his holiness and I understand the depth of my sinfulness in the light of his holiness, the awareness of my need drills down deeper and deeper until I cry out with conviction, 'Wretched man that I am! Who will deliver me from this body of death?' (Romans 7:24).

God leads us to himself through his word, not our merit. He draws our attention away from our striving to the joy and the grace that is to be found in Jesus Christ. As the realisation of our need grows, the joy in the finished work of Christ on the cross of Calvary grows still larger. The source of justifying faith is not on account of my merit, but on account of Christ, 'Thanks be to God through Jesus Christ our Lord!' (Romans 7:25).

The Revd Dr Henry Jansma *is Rector of All Souls Anglican Church, Cherry Hill NJ, Canon Theologian for the Missionary Diocese of CANA East, and Adjunct Professor at Reformed Episcopal Seminary, Blue Bell PA.*

Questions for Reflection

1. What does God think about the charitable giving of those who don't believe in him?
2. Why can't we be good without God?
3. Why is it so difficult for some to accept what this Article says?

Prayer

O God who cleanses the thoughts of our hearts by the inspiration of your Holy Spirit: give to us and all those we love, new hearts, that our lives may be a fragrant offering and sacrifice to you, through the merits of our saviour, Jesus Christ. *Amen.*

Bible Reading

Luke 17:5-10

The apostles said to the Lord, 'Increase our faith!' And the Lord said, 'If you had faith like a grain of mustard seed, you could say to this mulberry tree, 'Be uprooted and planted in the sea,' and it would obey you. 'Will any one of you who has a servant plowing or keeping sheep say to him when he has come in from the field, 'Come at once and recline at table'? Will he not rather say to him, "Prepare supper for me, and dress properly, and serve me while I eat and drink, and afterward you will eat and drink"? Does he thank the servant because he did what was commanded? So you also, when you have done all that you were commanded, say, "We are unworthy servants; we have only done what was our duty."'

Starter Question

Is it possible to be more righteous than God?

ARTICLE XIV

OF WORKS OF SUPEREROGATION

~

Voluntary Works besides, over, and above,
God's Commandments, which they call
Works of Supererogation, cannot be taught
without arrogancy and impiety: for by
them men do declare, that they do not only
render unto God as much as they are bound
to do, but that they do more for his sake,
than of bounden duty is required: whereas
Christ saith plainly, When ye have done
all that are commanded to you, say, We are
unprofitable servants.

ARTICLE XIV

5 00 years ago, being 'good enough' for God troubled Martin Luther. He realised, before and after his recovered insight into the gospel of St Paul, that he wasn't good enough. He felt the weight and burden of his sin (the theological category, not the psychological category of a supposed neurosis). He knew that he was unworthy and unable to be accepted by a holy God. Before his conversion, his life was a series of religious and moral attempts to get into, and stay in, God's good books. His attempts to satisfy the demands of a holy and righteous God were ineffective, and he knew it. He had no peace.

Then his Bible fell open at St Paul's letter to the Romans, where he discovered that someone else was completely righteous, impeccable, entirely holy and worthy. Christ had paid it all. And all that Martin had to do—and how he had desperately tried to 'do'!—was to relate to that someone, only by faith, getting into God's good books. This someone else was Jesus.

Luther had unearthed an idea (or an article of faith) from the debris created by the centuries-old dominance of a religious system which 'made you pay.' To get into and stay in God's good books required morality, sincerity, and ecclesiastical co-operation—a religious meritocracy. To remain there, it kept you paying, storing up God's favour for the spiritual 'rainy day', for you, your family or friends. This payment was metaphorical through giving of yourself in devotion and self-justification towards God. Moreover, and most provocatively to Luther, it was literal payment for indulgences to appease the unappeasable and insatiable divine. In pulling the barely alive child of justification 'by faith alone' from the rubble, Luther received life and peace.

Cranmer solidified this insight in our Articles, applying it fully. Faith in Christ both gets and keeps you saved, and it is this 'being kept' which is the concern of Article 14. Is there anything we need to do to secure our salvation in Christ? The Article on Supererogation comes within a unit on Christ and his exclusive, atoning work on behalf of his people. The Articles are thematically organised, moving from God to Christ, his salvation, people, and so on. They reflect Christian living. They deal with the realities of faith and they know the human heart. We need assurance.

This Article is quirky to twenty-first century readers. The word, supererogation, which is the subject of the Article is unfamiliar to us and the word has fallen into disuse. It simply means 'above and beyond our duty' religious works. However, the concept is very familiar to us and the remedy it deploys remains relevant for daily Christian living. Having been saved by Christ's grace through faith alone, we so continue to feel our unworthiness that we revert back to a modification of Luther's basic crisis: how do I remain good enough for God?

To answer that question we turn back to ourselves, making attempts to achieve and retain God's saving grace. Better and regular quiet times and more mystical religious experience. Increase spiritual activity—even praying for 24 hours, 7 days a week! We emphasise helping numerous old ladies across the road and the alleviation of all kinds of socio-economic problems. Each of these 'above and beyond our duty' religious works are certain to ensure God's smile and favour.

Sadly, this isn't too far from the answer which the medieval church gave. It is a medieval spirituality given an evangelical veneer. To stay in God's good books, prayers, self-denial, monastic orders, martyrdom, and an assortment of recommended works were considered 'spiritual brownie points.' They secured even more salvation, and accrued salvific interest on the bank balance of an individual's salvation. Just in case I (or a deceased family member) leak God's grace, I compensate and do something to top up my righteousness for those moments when I feel failure or experience distance from God. I make restitution for what I perceive to be lacking in God's grace towards me and my devotion towards him.

But, isn't this a classic case of sinful human arrogance? Article 14 points this out, saying that such works 'cannot be taught without arrogance and impiety.' We may think (even preach) that salvation is all of God, but act (and believe) as if it isn't. All of salvation comes from Christ's work on our behalf. Faith places us in Christ fully, firmly, finally, and forever. There is no need to fear when our trust is in Christ alone. He is sufficient and his forgiveness is unchanging.

This Article is one of the few with direct quotations from Scripture. It cites Luke 17:10, 'Christ saith plainly, "When ye have done all that are commanded to you, say, We are unprofitable servants."' A few verses before that, even mustard seed-sized faith, is fully effective. Calling on God in repentance and faith, with the feeblest and weakest of voices, brings salvation. The gospel is not only for unconverted sinners. It is also for converted sinners. Simply trust in Jesus. He really has done it all. There is nothing more to be done or that can be done, either by him or his people.

The Revd Trevor Johnston *is the Rector of All Saints, University Street, Belfast.*

QUESTIONS FOR REFLECTION

1. Is there some aspect of your Christian life where you are tempted to be proud that you are doing better than others?
2. How attractive is it when people think they are living above and beyond God's requirements?
3. Is this Article meant to beat us down into a cringing, servile attitude towards God?

PRAYER

Lord God Almighty, creator and preserver of all things and judge of all people: grant us the privilege and gift of faith, that we may know you, the only true and righteous God, and Jesus Christ, whom to serve is perfect freedom. *Amen.*

Bible Reading

1 John 1:5-10

This is the message we have heard from him and proclaim to you, that God is light, and in him is no darkness at all. If we say we have fellowship with him while we walk in darkness, we lie and do not practice the truth. But if we walk in the light, as he is in the light, we have fellowship with one another, and the blood of Jesus his Son cleanses us from all sin. If we say we have no sin, we deceive ourselves, and the truth is not in us. If we confess our sins, he is faithful and just to forgive us our sins and to cleanse us from all unrighteousness. If we say we have not sinned, we make him a liar, and his word is not in us.

Starter Question

Is it possible to be free from sin in the Christian life?

ARTICLE XV

OF CHRIST ALONE WITHOUT SIN

~

Christ in the truth of our nature was made like unto us in all things, sin only except, from which he was clearly void, both in his flesh, and in his spirit. He came to be the Lamb without spot, who, by sacrifice of himself once made, should take away the sins of the world, and sin, as Saint John saith, was not in him. But all we the rest, although baptized, and born again in Christ, yet offend in many things; and if we say we have no sin, we deceive ourselves, and the truth is not in us.

ARTICLE XV

The Apostle John wrote that 'If we say we have no sin, we deceive ourselves, and the truth is not in us' (1 John 1:8). We can't be confident that we will deceive anyone else. While they may not tell us to our face, most people who spend time with us would easily list some of the particular sins which we struggle with (or perhaps, more tellingly, don't struggle with). But we can deceive *ourselves*, and that is the pastoral brilliance of this Article's inclusion in our formularies.

PERFECTIONISM

Some might think Article 15 is superfluous: the perfection of Christ has been implied, at least, in Article 2, and Article 9 has told us that original sin continues to infect the regenerate believer. And yet, as the apostle John tells us, we find it all too easy to deceive ourselves about our ongoing fallen nature. Sin, in its very nature, is blinding, so we don't detect its presence. Pride whispers to us, and misdirects us, so we don't notice its residence in our hearts. We see part of Cranmer's theological and pastoral genius, therefore, in his determination in this Article to banish 'perfectionism' from the pews of Christ's Church.

Historically, perfectionism, which teaches that the Christian can achieve a level of sinless maturity in this life, has kept raising its ugly head. John's first letter implies it was present in the early church; at the time of the Reformation, it is likely that Cranmer was responding to a perception that certain Anabaptists were claiming sinless perfection (though this was, perhaps, a misunderstanding of their right call for disciples to *strive* for sinlessness). John Wesley, in the eighteenth century, famously spoke of entire sanctification, though he never claimed it for himself. More recently, certain movements have taught a second-blessing experience or an act of dedication which would achieve sinlessness.

These false teachings do have some elements which are to be commended: they often begin by taking seriously the call of Jesus to 'be perfect, as your heavenly Father is perfect.' (Matthew 5:48). They frequently grasp some aspects of the 'inaugurated eschatology' of the gospel, whereby Jesus, through his death and resurrection has dragged into the present some of the realities of the future age (or rather he has taken us, in union with him, into that future age). Thus, Christians are now *saints*, truly sanctified to God (1 Corinthians 6:11).

However, these teachings stumble because, while the believer is truly indwelt by the Spirit, they are simultaneously indwelt by sin (Romans 7:20). It is perhaps no surprise that 'Perfectionism Movements' tend to be short-lived. Their Achilles' heel is that while they may succeed in deceiving themselves for a time, most often by downgrading or limiting their definition of sin, the reality of ongoing sin is painfully plain to see.

Assumed Perfectionism

A full-orbed theological perfectionism is perhaps not a current danger for the Church. However, it may be that we are living in an age with a functional, or assumed, perfectionism. What would be the signs of such a deception? If we find ourselves shocked to discover sin in the lives of a fellow believer; if we bear a grudge easily; or simply permit past failings to damage our relationships with brothers and sisters: then, perhaps we would do well to take the teaching of Article 15 to heart.

Furthermore, the heart that struggles to forgive another Christian is a heart that is unaware of its own need for forgiveness from God (Matthew 18:21-35), or, in other words, a heart which believes the lie of perfectionism. Equally, the heart that will not accept loving rebuke from a fellow Christian has, most likely, swallowed the bait of perfectionist teaching. This last symptom seems to be endemic in our churches.

Each of us has what has been described as our own 'internal, personal defence lawyer', who instinctively leaps to defend us whenever we feel the mildest criticism. This may manifest itself in excuse-making, or bristling, or deflection, or even self-pity. But the heart that has truly absorbed the life-giving truth of Article 15 will silence the defence lawyer and humbly welcome the loving challenge of a Christian brother or sister. The wise believer will know they need this kind of fellowship, even, if possible, on a daily basis (Hebrews 3:12-14).

One further evidence of an assumed perfectionism would be a lack of any discussion of sin, as part of a larger pastoral or theological position. In Church debates about human sexuality, for example, one of the most troubling elements is when there is a notable absence of any consideration of the Fall, of indwelling sin, or of total depravity (whereby sin corrupts every aspect of us, including our desires and our minds). This omission severely compromises the conclusions that are drawn.

The antidote to this assumed perfectionism would be a healthy confessional life. It is odd that this liturgical element has disappeared from some of our churches. As well as making corporate confession, we would do well regularly to confess our sins privately before God in concrete, meaningful ways, which are personal and specific. We would do well to confess our sins to each other: to invite others to speak into our lives; to ask them to pray for us; to make our prayer requests not (just) about my difficult children, but about my short temper; not (just) about my tight finances but about my instinctive envy and self-pity; not (just) about my difficult boss but also about my proud, argumentative spirit.

DIMINISHING JESUS

However, the greatest problem with perfectionist teaching is that it diminishes the Lord Jesus Christ. Article 15 captures the profound difference between his sinless perfection and our sinful state. There is a vast chasm separating him from us. Perfectionism reduces this Grand Canyon to a small ditch; it leads the believer to make light of Jesus' sinlessness: 'it's not such a big deal, for in the end, I can be sinless too.' Whereas, the believer who has drunk deeply from the waters of Article 15 recognises the pervasive, putrid pull of sin and so is overwhelmed by the powerful purity of the Saviour.

There can be a temptation to assume that Jesus' perfection was easy for him, but Scripture will not permit that (Hebrews 5:8). The Garden of Gethsemane reveals to us the terrible cost of sinlessness (Mark 14:36). The person who gives up on a marathon after half a mile cannot claim to know the true pain of long distance running. In the same way, none of us truly know the pain of resisting sin. Jesus alone has endured to the end and come out victorious. Article 15 leads us to marvel at the beauty of Jesus' character, and increasingly so, for as we grow in the faith, so the Spirit reveals to us more of the gulf between his perfection and our sinfulness.

Finally, perfectionism, does not simply diminish the moral beauty of the Lord Jesus. It also diminishes the horror of the cross and the astonishing love of God revealed there. God made him, who knew no sin, to be sin for us. (2 Corinthians 5:21). If a bride should stop on the way into the church, take her pristine white wedding dress, and use it to wipe the vomit from the face of a homeless drug addict, we would be repulsed—unless we happen to be the addict. What Christ has done for us is infinitely greater. In his moral perfection he has taken onto himself all the filth of our sin, so that we might be sanctified and, one day in glory, be perfect like him.

'Beloved, we are God's children now, and what we will be has not yet appeared; but we know that when he appears we shall be like him, because we shall see him as he is. And everyone who thus hopes in him, purifies himself, as he is pure' (1 John 3:2-3).

The Revd Ben Thompson *is Pioneer Minister for Moreton-in-Marsh and a PhD candidate at Queen's University, Belfast.*

QUESTIONS FOR REFLECTION

1. What signs should I watch for that could indicate I am deceiving myself about my ongoing sinfulness?
2. What are the dangers of teaching 'perfectionism'?
3. Do you confess your sins corporately in church, and privately in prayer to God? What would help you avoid the trap of saying these words thoughtlessly, with hearts that are far from God (Mark 7:6)?

PRAYER

Almighty God, to whom the angels cry, 'Holy, Holy, Holy': assist us by your Spirit to put to death the misdeeds of our bodies and minds, that as we follow your spotless Son, we might trust in his once and for all sacrifice for our sins which alone can give us true hope. In Jesus name. *Amen.*

Bible Reading

2 Timothy 2:22-26

So flee youthful passions and pursue righteousness,
faith, love, and peace, along with those who call on the
Lord from a pure heart. Have nothing to do with foolish, ignorant controversies; you know that they breed
quarrels. And the Lord's servant must not be quarrelsome but kind to everyone, able to teach, patiently enduring evil, correcting his opponents with gentleness.
God may perhaps grant them repentance leading to a
knowledge of the truth, and they may come to their
senses and escape from the snare of the devil, after being
captured by him to do his will.

Starter Question

*What is our part and what is God's part in restoring people who
have moved away from true faith?*

ARTICLE XVI

OF SIN AFTER BAPTISM

~

Not every deadly sin willingly committed after Baptism is sin against the Holy Ghost, and unpardonable. Wherefore the grant of repentance is not to be denied to such as fall into sin after Baptism. After we have received the Holy Ghost, we may depart from grace given, and fall into sin, and by the grace of God we may arise again, and amend our lives. And therefore they are to be condemned, which say, they can no more sin as long as they live here, or deny the place of forgiveness to such as truly repent.

ARTICLE XVI

Recently, I was helping with our church holiday club over half-term. On one of the days, following the main teaching slot, I was chatting in my group with two eight-year-old boys. We were talking about sin and the need for Jesus to save us. In trying to help them understand the teaching I asked them 'Do you think you could get through the whole day without sinning, without doing anything wrong?' One clearly thought he could and explained how! It took a little time and some challenging questions for him to begin to think that maybe he couldn't quite make it through a whole day sinless, even if he tried very hard.

He was not alone in thinking he could be perfect. Over the centuries people have wrongly taught that you can be perfect this side of heaven. I guess most of us know that our experience of life after conversion does not reflect that.

Such a teaching can raise all kinds of difficulties pastorally as well as being unbiblical. I have come across those who struggle with assurance about whether they are truly saved: 'How can I really be a Christian if I keep on sinning?' Some have done things which they think puts them beyond the reach of God, that they can't be forgiven. 'Surely if the Holy Spirit now dwells in me I shouldn't sin, so perhaps he doesn't.' Such thoughts are not unique to the twenty-first century.

BEYOND HELP?

One error rife at the Reformation was the revival of the old idea from Novatian, in the third century, that serious sins committed after baptism (conversion) could not be forgiven. But it was also taught by some that it was impossible for the regenerate to sin. So apart from the unforgivable sin against the Holy Spirit, is there any sin so serious that can put someone beyond forgiveness? This is slightly different language from what we use today, perhaps, but we face the same issues.

The Thirty-nine Articles continue to speak into a fallen world, dealing with such false teaching and helping point us back to biblical teaching and the amazing grace of God. So how does Article 16 speak into the world today?

It can be helpful in the pastoral situations we have already mentioned. Article 16 helps point to the reality that we will sin after we have come to faith, but those sins will not put us beyond God's forgiveness. As we look back, we can see how God has changed and is changing us through his Holy Spirit. No, we won't reach perfection this side of heaven, but we shouldn't lose heart either as we seem to struggle with some repeating sin, because we know that God is at work. 'And we who with unveiled faces all reflect the Lord's glory, are being transformed into his likeness with ever increasing glory, which comes from the Lord, who is the Spirit' (2 Corinthians 3:18).

Talking about sin is not perhaps the best topic for everyday conversation. Surely if you must talk about religion, people say, then talk about how loving God is! People don't want to talk about sin. But aren't we short-changing people if we don't talk about sin? If we don't understand the role of sin in our lives, then we can't fully understand that amazing love God has for us in sending Jesus to die in our place; the fact that we can do nothing to sort out sin; that even when we come to faith and sin over and over again, we can come in repentance to God and he forgives us time and time again; and how through the work of the Holy Spirit he is changing us, so that we might one day be presented to Christ 'as a radiant church, without stain, or wrinkle or any other blemish, but holy and blameless' (Ephesians 5:27).

Works in Progress

This group of Articles (Articles 12-16) are actually very encouraging. They are realistic and help us see where we start from—the human condition. And as we understand our sin and see our need for rescue, so we appreciate even more deeply the grace and goodness of God in adopting us into his family and continuing to work in our lives.

We are works in progress. So yes, we do sin even though we have been made righteous through Christ's blood. But we have this certain hope that one day when we stand before God he will see us perfect. All possible because of what God has done, not something we have earned which therefore could be lost. What an amazing truth!

Take some time today to thank God that he has rescued us from the power of sin and is, by his Holy Spirit changing us to be more Christ-like, so that one day we can stand before him holy and blameless.

The Revd Clare Hendry *is Associate Minister at Grace Church, Muswell Hill and formerly taught pastoral counselling at Oak Hill Theological College, London.*

QUESTIONS FOR REFLECTION

1. How might you or your church give a false impression about the impossibility of repentance?
2. How important is forgiveness in your church life?
3. When did you last 'arise again and amend your life' as a result of hearing God's word?

PRAYER

Merciful God, who calls all those who have erred and strayed from your ways like lost sheep to repent and return to your loving arms: grant us repentance and a knowledge of your truth that we may ever hold fast the promise of forgiveness in Jesus Christ our Lord. *Amen.*

Bible Reading

Romans 8:28-34

And we know that for those who love God all things work together for good, for those who are called according to his purpose. For those whom he foreknew he also predestined to be conformed to the image of his Son, in order that he might be the firstborn among many brothers. And those whom he predestined he also called, and those whom he called he also justified, and those whom he justified he also glorified.

What then shall we say to these things? If God is for us, who can be against us? He who did not spare his own Son but gave him up for us all, how will he not also with him graciously give us all things? Who shall bring any charge against God's elect? It is God who justifies. Who is to condemn?

Starter Question

Is predestination a scary, comforting, or confusing doctrine for you?

ARTICLE XVII

OF PREDESTINATION AND ELECTION

~

Predestination to Life is the everlasting purpose of God, whereby (before the foundations of the world were laid) he hath constantly decreed by his counsel secret to us, to deliver from curse and damnation those whom he hath chosen in Christ out of mankind, and to bring them by Christ to everlasting salvation, as vessels made to honour. Wherefore, they which be endued with so excellent a benefit of God be called according to God's purpose by his Spirit working in due season: they through Grace obey the calling: they be justified freely: they be made sons of God by adoption: they be made like the image of his only-begotten Son Jesus Christ: they walk religiously in good works, and at length, by God's mercy, they attain to everlasting felicity.

As the godly consideration of Predestination, and
our Election in Christ, is full of sweet, pleasant, and
unspeakable comfort to godly persons, and such
as feel in themselves the working of the Spirit of
Christ, mortifying the works of the flesh, and their
earthly members, and drawing up their mind to
high and heavenly things, as well because it doth
greatly establish and confirm their faith of eternal
Salvation to be enjoyed through Christ, as because
it doth fervently kindle their love towards God: So,
for curious and carnal persons, lacking the Spirit
of Christ, to have continually before their eyes the
sentence of God's Predestination, is a most dangerous
downfall, whereby the Devil doth thrust them either
into desperation, or into wretchlessness of most
unclean living, no less perilous than desperation.
Furthermore, we must receive God's promises in
such wise, as they be generally set forth to us in holy
Scripture: and, in our doings, that Will of God is to
be followed, which we have expressly declared unto us
in the Word of God.

ARTICLE XVII

I s God for you or against you? And if he is for you, to what
extent is he for you?
On the other hand, would you like to be more confident in
your faith? And more loving towards God?

Article 17 is the longest Article by a considerable margin. Careful explanation was clearly necessary. But the doctrine was nothing
new. Augustine of Hippo had taught the biblical doctrine over
1000 years before our Article was written.

Despite its length, it is just four sentences.

GLORY TO GOD ALONE

The first sentence is a straightforward, uncompromising, and positive statement of the doctrine: God has chosen those who will be
eternally saved. This choice predates everything and its effects last
forever. In Christ, the elect are saved forever from condemnation:
chosen in him, redeemed in him, and certain to inherit in him
(Ephesians 1:3-14). There is never any variation in this purpose of
God. God has not told us who the chosen are, but he unfailingly
brings them to the place of honour.

The second sentence describes how this purpose works out on
the ground in history in the individual believer. It may take a
long time, with many ups and downs along the way, but in the
end the elect individual experiences the invitation of the gospel

and accepts it, enjoys their new justified status, and continues in Christ-like good works until they go to be with Christ forever. But the Article repeatedly makes clear that from start to finish at every step it is God who effects his purpose in the chosen. He does so by the Spirit, through grace, freely, by his mercy. We certainly obey and walk, but we do so because of God's powerful and unmerited work in us.

So as a Christian, is God for you? Certainly! To what extent is God for you? Completely! It is impossible to imagine a gospel where God more completely plans, executes, and fulfils salvation for us.

Every Christian knows that we are saved by God's grace. Even the Church of Rome has never denied that God freely gives what is undeserved. But the Article sets forth the only theological system which expresses salvation by God's grace *alone*. Deciding to trust and follow Christ is the best decision anyone can make. But I did not so decide because I was clever, or more discerning than my neighbour, or more able than some others. I decided because in God's kindness to me, in his determination to bring his elect in Christ to glory, he caused me to. God is so for us, that he ensures not even we, with all our corruption, can separate ourselves from his love in Christ Jesus (Romans 8:28-39).

And so it is plain why all the glory belongs to God. The true gospel of grace alone can only result in glory to the God who alone gives that grace. We should be moved to praise God for his immeasurable generosity to us in Christ: chosen in him, redeemed in him, and certain to inherit in him. And we should also find the greatest comfort when we consider this doctrine.

Unspeakable Comfort

And so the Article naturally turns to its third sentence, pointing us to how unspeakably comforting this doctrine is to the believer. But in expounding the healthy use of this doctrine, we are also warned about its destructive use.

If the preceding paragraphs are worth anything, then you, the believer, should be growing in assurance that you are truly saved and secure in Christ forever. We are not still believing because we are so good at holding onto God, but because God is so good at holding on to us. He is unfailing in fulfilling his purpose in Christ for us.

In life, I am always more likely to trust someone who I know is genuinely on my side. Proper appreciation of just how much God is for us in Christ should make us trust him more (and more readily) than anyone or anything else. Similarly, I am always more likely to love someone who has been good to me for no reason other than their love for me. In love he predestined us for redemption and glory. How this should lift our affections to him!

So would you like to be more confident in your faith? And more loving towards God? Then think on and pray through this doctrine.

CAREFUL APPLICATION

There is a warning though. As we teach biblical doctrine, we must apply biblical doctrine as the Bible does. The Bible only applies the doctrine of election and predestination to encourage God's already believing people. The doctrine of election is not itself the gospel of grace alone that is to be preached to all the world. It defends that gospel from ideas of human merit, and impresses upon the believer the absolute security we enjoy in the gospel. 'Are you chosen in Christ?' is a constructive question for the believer, but an uncaring opening question in evangelism.

It is, however, an encouragement to keep preaching the gospel of grace. Christians often get this the wrong way round, but as a preacher myself, if people's salvation depended on them or me, I would have given up a long time ago. But it is God who effectually calls out and saves his people.

In its final sentence the Article calls for repentance and faith. It humbles the objector to this doctrine and keeps us away from false assurance. Every elect person will, in due time, repent and believe. There is no evidence of any saving work of God in someone without repentance and faith, whatever they might claim.

So if you are worried about your election, repent and believe in Jesus Christ. If you are confident of your election, repent and believe in Jesus Christ. Then we will praise and love him in eternal security.

The Revd Paul Darlington *is the Vicar of Holy Trinity, Oswestry, Chairman of the Church Society council, and author of Evangelical Ministry in a Non-evangelical Parish.*

QUESTIONS FOR REFLECTION

1. Why is predestination not an excuse for passivity or ungodliness?
2. Is our predestination based on God foreseeing our future good works and potential?
3. Why do we still need to evangelise if God has already chosen some people to receive salvation?

PRAYER

Sovereign Lord, who works all things in conformity to your good and perfect will: keep us in your unfailing love; and as those chosen to be holy and blameless in your sight, help us make our calling and election sure. For the glory of your holy name, through Jesus Christ our Lord. *Amen.*

Bible Reading

John 14:1-6

Let not your hearts be troubled. Believe in God; believe also in me. In my Father's house are many rooms. If it were not so, would I have told you that I go to prepare a place for you? And if I go and prepare a place for you, I will come again and will take you to myself, that where I am you may be also. And you know the way to where I am going." Thomas said to him, "Lord, we do not know where you are going. How can we know the way?" Jesus said to him, "I am the way, and the truth, and the life. No one comes to the Father except through me."

Starter Question

What would you say to someone who said all religions were simply different paths up the same mountain?

ARTICLE XVIII

OF OBTAINING ETERNAL SALVATION ONLY BY THE NAME OF CHRIST

They also are to be had accursed that presume to say, That every man shall be saved by the Law or Sect which he professeth, so that he be diligent to frame his life according to that Law, and the light of Nature. For holy Scripture doth set out unto us only the Name of Jesus Christ, whereby men must be saved.

ARTICLE XVIII

There is no more important question in our day and in the church than that of other religions. The question goes something like this: 'Since there are so many different religions in the world, aren't there many different ways to God? I know that those of other religions are very sincere in their beliefs, and they are also very good people, so, surely all those who live sincere lives will be led to God?' People say that there are many paths up the one mountain. Indeed, many believe that the most offensive and nonsensical thing that anyone can say is that there is only one way to God. All spiritual truth, we are told, is plural and relative.

Yet, we know that to say 'all that matters is sincerity' is simply not true in other areas of life. It really does matter that the pilot of your plane knows how to fly a plane and the way to its destination. In this case, sincerity is just not enough. After all, when we consider the identity of God in different religions, we see that religions contradict one another. Christians believe that God is one but Trinity; Islam believes that God is one, but definitely not Trinity; Hinduism believes that God is many; and others, including Buddhists believe that God does not exist as a personal being. Many in our culture believe in a divine 'force', but not much more. So, which one is right?

It is here that Article 18 is so very helpful and relevant, even though, in the sixteenth century, the only non-Christian religions the Reformers generally knew about were Judaism and Islam, and the only sects were some odd anti-Trinitarians. The Article also stresses that it is Christ alone who saves, not, as in the Roman Catholic church, that you can add in the Virgin Mary somehow to Christ's work as mediator and redeemer. So, let's have a look at the Article in detail.

THE ERROR CONDEMNED

Article 18 points out that we cannot be saved either by the diligent sincerity of the beliefs 'we professeth' or our personal 'sect' or religion. Indeed we are 'accursed' if we believe such things. Religions cannot save us nor can the sense human beings have by looking at the light of nature or conscience in our hearts that there is a God.

Article 18 is in agreement with the Bible. Paul speaks in Romans 1:18-23 about the human problem to which the gospel is the solution. He says that even though God clearly revealed himself to us in creation, people have rejected this knowledge of him. And so 'they are without excuse.' Further, we have exchanged the true God for idols (that is, religion, our own ideas about God) and 'exchanged the glory of the immortal God for images.' And so, Paul says, we are all under 'the wrath of God.'

So how can we have saving knowledge of God?

THE TRUTH EXPLAINED

Article 18 explains that the only way we can be saved is 'the Name of Jesus Christ.' What the Article means is that you have to trust in Jesus Christ alone for salvation. Why does the Article assert something so offensive to our society? Because the Bible says so.

First, in the prophet Isaiah, God says that '*I am* the LORD, and there is no other, besides me there is no God' (Isaiah 45:5). Notice here that the God of the Bible is the true God, and also that other 'gods' (which the Bible calls 'idols') are not the true God.

Secondly, Jesus, in his farewell teaching to his disciples, the night before the cross, in John 14:6, echoes Isaiah and reveals to us the way to God and heaven. He says: '*I am* the Way, and the Truth, and the Life; no one comes to the Father except through me.' As God come to earth, Jesus has the right to tell us the way to heaven.

It is very important to see what Jesus says: He is the definite and singular 'Way' to God (not 'a way'). He is the absolute 'Truth' about God and from God (not 'a truth about God'), and he is the true 'Life' of God and the giver of eternal life (not 'a nice way to live').

Crucially, Jesus also goes onto the negative: 'no one comes to the Father except through me.' That is, the only way for human beings to know God as our Father in heavenly life is through faith and knowledge in Jesus Christ as God and Saviour (John 20:30-31).

Now, I was not brought up in a Christian family. I was an Indian Zoroastrian. I believed in many ways to God. But then some Christian friends told me that I was going to hell unless I had faith in Jesus, because he is the only Way. I was very offended by that message, but I read the message of John 14:6. I knew I had to either accept this Jesus or reject him. But I knew that Jesus had risen from the dead and so I said, like Thomas, to this risen Lord Jesus 'My Lord and my God' (John 20:29).

Article 18 also points us to Acts 4:12, to which it alludes: 'For Holy Scripture doth set out unto us only the name of Jesus Christ whereby men must be saved.' In Acts 4, Peter preaches to the Jewish leaders and says in verse 12, 'And there is salvation in no one else, for there is no other name under heaven given among men by which we must be saved.' Here Peter asserts that there is no other saviour except Jesus Christ. Why? Because only Jesus saves, since only Jesus died for our sins.

Secondly, Peter tells us that God (that is what Peter means by 'heaven') has appointed and named his Son, Jesus, as the only one with the authority and power to save and rescue sinful human beings.

Lastly, notice that the name of Jesus is, according to God's divine decree, the name 'by which we must be saved.' There can be no human option here like, 'I will choose to be saved in my own way or by my own god or religion.' Rather Peter says, 'No, God has decreed and fixed that we *must* be saved only through faith in Christ.'

CONCLUSION

So, to conclude, the Article rightly says that we can only be saved by faith in Christ alone, and not by sincerity, religion, or nature. It is a breath-taking statement to make. It is a counter-cultural truth to proclaim. But it also means that we can have assurance that we have Christ and are saved, and that we can tell people of other faiths (like me before conversion) that there is only one Way to be saved, because Jesus Christ is the unique and exclusive Saviour.

The Revd Dr Rohintan Mody *is Lecturer in New Testament at the Evangelical Theological College of Asia and the author of Empty and Evil: The worship of other faiths in 1 Corinthians 8-10 and today.*

QUESTIONS FOR REFLECTION

1. Why is sincerity no guide to truth?
2. 'It is not very humble or loving to say Jesus is the only way to God.' How would you reply?
3. Should Christians worship together with those of other religions?

PRAYER

Lord Jesus Christ, you are the way, and the truth, and the life and there is no other name by which we must be saved: enable us by your Spirit to worship you in humility and truth that we may spread the gospel of your grace to every corner of your world, for the glory of your name. *Amen.*

BIBLE READING

Ephesians 5:25-32

Husbands, love your wives, as Christ loved the church and gave himself up for her, that he might sanctify her, having cleansed her by the washing of water with the word, so that he might present the church to himself in splendour, without spot or wrinkle or any such thing, that she might be holy and without blemish. In the same way husbands should love their wives as their own bodies. He who loves his wife loves himself. For no one ever hated his own flesh, but nourishes and cherishes it, just as Christ does the church, because we are members of his body. 'Therefore a man shall leave his father and mother and hold fast to his wife, and the two shall become one flesh.' This mystery is profound, and I am saying that it refers to Christ and the church.

STARTER QUESTION

What does Christ want the church to be, and how does he accomplish this?

ARTICLE XIX

OF THE CHURCH

~

The visible Church of Christ is a congregation of faithful men, in the which the pure Word of God is preached, and the Sacraments be duly ministered according to Christ's ordinance in all those things that of necessity are requisite to the same. As the Church of Jerusalem, Alexandria, and Antioch, have erred; so also the Church of Rome hath erred, not only in their living and manner of Ceremonies, but also in matters of Faith.

Article xix

To many Christians this Article may seem superfluous. After all, 'church' is the place where we go for hymns, sermons, Communion, and the occasional wedding or funeral. Right? The Reformers knew that the outworking of their theology, based squarely on the sufficiency and authority of the Scriptures, was a direct challenge to Rome and the papacy. It was therefore essential to say what constituted a true church and what did not. Article 19 is similar to that of Article 7 of the Augsburg Confession of 1530 and reflects a shared Protestant consensus that Rome's teaching on the Church needed to be reformed.

A Faithful People

a. Visible

The Article assumes that the Church is to be a visible company of believers in Jesus Christ. This is the whole tenor of the New Testament: Offences should be told to the church (Matthew 18:17); the Church is like a light that cannot be hidden (Matthew 5:14); many were added to the number of believers by the apostles' teaching (Acts 2:47). This is all inexplicable unless it refers to a visible society of Christians.

Article 26 explicitly states that, as in the parable of the wheat and the tares, in the visible church 'the evil are ever mingled with the good.' Cranmer was well aware of this visible/invisible Church distinction, as is evident in his *Thirteen Articles* (1538), where we read that 'true believers, who really believe in Christ the Head' make up the invisible Church, and the visible Church comprises 'all who are baptised in Christ, who have not openly denied him nor been lawfully and by his Word excommunicated.'

b. Congregational

Cranmer was probably thinking of 'congregation' as not just a single group of local believers, but as a larger, regional or even national body. This larger meaning is also suggested by the later mention of the ancient patriarchates (the Church of Jerusalem, the Church of Alexandria etc). The biblical doctrine of the Church is a corrective against an individualism which focuses narrowly on personal wishes and the end goal of self-satisfaction. The New Testament imagery of a body and building (1 Corinthians 12:12-31; Ephesians 1:22-23, 2:19-22; 1 Peter 2:4-10) emphasises this corporate dimension.

c. Faithful

'Faithful' has here to be seen as all those who profess and call themselves Christians. As Gerald Bray puts it, 'We are not dealing here with a club full of dedicated supporters, but with a fellowship of those who share the same fundamental beliefs.' In the Church of England we are painfully aware that this is not always so. We must insist that right beliefs are placed before any fixation with buildings or any sort of institutional loyalty or unity.

MARKS OF THE TRUE CHURCH

a. Word

The Reformers were strong advocates for proper theological training for legally authorised ministers (Article 23), so they would actually know what the pure word of God is, and could also preach that message. Non-preaching, 'dumb' ministers were a contradiction in terms. Today, we should consider carefully the difference between a five minute homily and consistent expositional preaching as means to spiritually nourish a congregation of God's people. Is preaching and Bible study a priority, or just an optional extra which people tolerate, but do not value?

b. Sacrament

The two dominical sacraments of baptism and the Lord's supper (Article 25) also have to be administered in a way which is both loyal to the Scriptures and avoids error. The Reformers therefore fought against abuses: private communion denied the corporate fellowship of Christ's Church and encouraged superstition; denying the laity the cup was against the Lord's command; indiscriminate baptism of infants downplayed the importance of personal faith and suggested automatic salvation on being baptised. If sacraments are not administered properly in the church, or dispensed with altogether (e.g. Quakers, Salvation Army), then the nature of the gospel is obscured and people's eternal salvation could be at stake.

This Article should make us consider the advice we give, for example, to students seeking a church during term-time, or a retired couple moving to a new area. Loyalty to a local parish church, social activities, or style of music can never replace a proper use of word and sacrament as God's appointed means of grace.

These key characteristics or 'marks' of the visible church also have a polemical function in excluding the necessity of accepting the authority of the Bishop of Rome. The Church of England, displaying these marks, must therefore be seen to be part of the true Church, despite rejecting papal authority under Henry VIII in 1534 and again under Elizabeth I in 1559. Article 19 needs to be understood in this anti-Roman way, although the definition does not make this intention explicit.

c. Discipline?

It should be noted in passing that many Protestants added a third 'mark' of the true Church, ecclesiastical discipline. Some see this as included in the sacraments being 'duly ministered', with the necessary requirements of due examination, excommunication etc. In addition to the *Westminster Confession of Faith* (1646), other Anglican formularies include ecclesiastical discipline as a mark, including the Homily for Whitsunday (1563), and Alexander Nowell's *Catechism* (1570). Nowell makes the distinction between word and sacrament as 'the chief and necessary marks of the church' and discipline as a mark of a 'well ordered' church.

No Church is Perfect

a. Every church can err

The Reformers insisted that Rome had indeed erred, although it should be remembered that papal infallibility was not officially established until the nineteenth century. The Papacy insisted that Rome had been preserved from error throughout history, in contrast to both the Eastern churches and the Protestants.

The purpose of Article 19 is illuminated when one examines the *Reformatio Legum Ecclesiasticarum* (1552) the abortive attempt at reforming Canon Law in the English Church. It talks of 'the insanity of those who think that the Roman church was founded on a rock of such a kind that it has neither erred nor can err'. The Article is therefore very similar in its intention, as Martin Davie says, 'to provide a definition of the Church that would refute the arguments of those who maintained that the visible Church had to be under the authority of the Church of Rome.'

The Article towards its close mentions the three historic patriarchates of the Eastern Church, 'Jerusalem, Alexandria, and Antioch', powerful churches, which, though founded by apostles, had still fallen into error. The actual errors are not spelt out, but have generally been taken as doctrinal errors regarding Christology. Their examples should serve as a warning that no church, including Rome, is perfect. We must never presume that sound teaching will be either popular or inevitably preserved, especially under such intense pressure today of liberal teaching from within and an aggressively secular culture from without.

b. A necessary Reformation

In this 500th anniversary of the Reformation we should not be embarrassed to agree with the Reformers in their rejection of the errors that had crept into the medieval Church. The Church of England is a Protestant church, not some sort of *via media* (middle way) between Protestantism and Roman Catholicism. Article 19 is a useful reminder that the laudable quest for Church unity should never take precedence over true doctrine.

Although the Reformers held Rome to be in error, Rome was still generally considered to be part of the true Church—the Article does, after all, refer to 'the Church of Rome.' Richard Hooker, in his *Laws of Ecclesiastical Polity* (III.i.10), reacts strongly against the Puritan position of totally rejecting Rome: 'we dare not communicate concerning sundry her gross and grievous abominations, yet touching those main parts of Christian truth wherein they consistently still persist, we gladly acknowledge them to be of the family of Jesus Christ.'

The Revd Dr Andrew Cinnamond *is Vicar of St Lawrence, Lechlade and the author of What Matters in Reforming the Church? Puritan Grievances under Elizabeth I.*

QUESTIONS FOR REFLECTION

1. Why is it important to acknowledge that the church is more than just your local congregation?
2. Why is the word of God so important for the church of God?
3. How does it change our ways of doing things if we believe that 'the church can err'?

PRAYER

Heavenly Father, you have built your people, the church, on the foundation of the apostles and prophets, Christ Jesus himself being the cornerstone: by your Spirit, build us up and knit us together by your most holy word so that through us your manifold wisdom might be made known in the heavenly places, through Jesus Christ our Saviour. *Amen.*

BIBLE READING

Matthew 15:1-9

Then Pharisees and scribes came to Jesus from Jerusalem and said, 'Why do your disciples break the tradition of the elders? For they do not wash their hands when they eat.' He answered them, 'And why do you break the commandment of God for the sake of your tradition? For God commanded, 'Honour your father and your mother,' and, 'Whoever reviles father or mother must surely die.' But you say, 'If anyone tells his father or his mother, 'What you would have gained from me is given to God,' he need not honour his father.' So for the sake of your tradition you have made void the word of God. You hypocrites! Well did Isaiah prophesy of you, when he said:

"This people honours me with their lips,
>   but their heart is far from me;
> in vain do they worship me, teaching
>   as doctrines the commandments of men.'"

STARTER QUESTION

What limitations ought there to be on church traditions?

ARTICLE XX

OF THE AUTHORITY OF THE CHURCH

~

The Church hath power to decree Rites or Ceremonies, and authority in Controversies of Faith: And yet it is not lawful for the Church to ordain any thing that is contrary to God's Word written, neither may it so expound one place of Scripture, that it be repugnant to another. Wherefore, although the Church be a witness and a keeper of holy Writ, yet, as it ought not to decree any thing against the same, so besides the same ought it not to enforce any thing to be believed for necessity of Salvation.

Article xx

A rticle 20 is only a short paragraph and yet it packs a powerful and highly relevant punch for today's Church.

This Article deals with the perennially vital question of the Church's authority. It articulates historic Anglicanism's careful, clear, and nuanced wisdom on this subject. It demonstrates convincingly J. I. Packer's comment that, 'The Thirty-nine Articles seem not only to catch the substance and spirit of biblical Christianity superbly well but also provide as apt a model of the way to confess the faith in a divided Christendom as the world has yet seen.'

The Anglican Doctrine of Scripture

Firstly, the Article gives an appropriate weight to tradition and the freedom of the Church. The Church has the right to develop culturally appropriate forms of worship. The Article allows that the Church as a body can make decisions and judgments in matters of controversy and disagreement. Scripture is 'sufficient' but not 'exhaustive.'

However, secondly and most importantly, Article 20 makes it crystal clear that Anglicanism affirms the supreme authority of Scripture. 'It is not lawful for the Church to ordain anything that is contrary to God's Word written... it ought not to decree any thing against the same.' The Church sits under the authority of Scripture, neither above it nor equal to it.

Thirdly, the Article understands the 'unity of Scripture' and that it does not contradict itself, therefore we must not interpret or expound any part of Scripture in a way that contradicts other parts of Scripture. Article 7 is particularly relevant here, because Anglicanism recognises the progressive nature of God's unfolding plan of salvation. Scripture's own internal authority explains why it is that the ceremonial laws and civil regulations given in the Old Testament are no longer binding but the moral law is. So for example in Mark 7:19, Mark explains that Jesus declared all foods clean, Scripture itself giving authority for such a change.

Fourthly, the Article implicitly recognises the importance of 'Systematic Theology.' The only way in which we can avoid expounding one part of Scripture in a way that contradicts another, is if we have an understanding of the whole.

Fifthly, consider the Church's relationship to Scripture here. The Church is a 'witness' and a 'keeper' of Scripture. As a witness it testifies to the truth that the Bible is God's word proclaiming the gospel of salvation. And as a keeper it is called (as a General Synod paper on the subject put it) to 'keep the biblical canon whole and entire and pass it on down the generations' (GS 1748B). The Church does not have authority over Scripture but is to bear witness to Scripture's authority.

ERRORS TO BE AVOIDED

This Article guards against two errors:

i. *Detracting from Scripture.* To ordain anything contrary to God's word is to ignore and reject its authoritative teaching.

ii. *Adding to Scripture.* The 'sufficiency of Scripture' means that the Church must not add to the biblical gospel anything as a requirement for salvation.

IMPLICATIONS

And so finally, we must note the implications of this:

- If all of Scripture is authoritative, we cannot, for example, disregard the teaching of the apostle Paul if the same commands are not found on the lips of Jesus. Nor can we regard them as less significant.

• Every debate, discussion and decision made in the local church, deanery, diocese, or General Synod ought to be primarily concerned to discern and correctly interpret the teaching of Scripture on any particular issue and to be governed by that.

The Revd Dr Mark Pickles *is the Director of Anglican Ministry Training at Oak Hill Theological College, London and co-author with Lee Gatiss and Mike Ovey of Be Faithful: Remaining Steadfast in the Church of England Today.*

Questions for Reflection

1. How do you decide what to believe when you find apparent contradictions in the Bible?
2. How can the church ensure that it does not go against scripture in its traditions?
3. What would you say to those who assert that 'the church gave us the Bible so the church can re-write or ignore the Bible'?

Prayer

God of peace and author of our salvation, who will soon crush Satan under our feet: take from us all ignorance, hardness of heart, and contempt for your word, that we may serve not our own appetites and desires but the Lord Christ, who is alive and reigns with you and the Holy Spirit, one God, now and forever. *Amen.*

Bible Reading

Acts 15:6-11, 13-15

The apostles and the elders were gathered together to consider this matter. And after there had been much debate, Peter stood up and said to them, 'Brothers, you know that in the early days God made a choice among you, that by my mouth the Gentiles should hear the word of the gospel and believe. And God, who knows the heart, bore witness to them, by giving them the Holy Spirit just as he did to us, and he made no distinction between us and them, having cleansed their hearts by faith. Now, therefore, why are you putting God to the test by placing a yoke on the neck of the disciples that neither our fathers nor we have been able to bear? But we believe that we will be saved through the grace of the Lord Jesus, just as they will.' … James replied, 'Brothers, listen to me. Simeon has related how God first visited the Gentiles, to take from them a people for his name. And with this the words of the prophets agree…'

Starter Question

How did the Council of Jerusalem in Acts 15 make its decision about whether to circumcise Gentile converts?

ARTICLE XXI

OF THE AUTHORITY OF GENERAL COUNCILS

~

General Councils may not be gathered together without the commandment and will of Princes. And when they be gathered together, (forasmuch as they be an assembly of men, whereof all be not governed with the Spirit and Word of God,) they may err, and sometimes have erred, even in things pertaining unto God. Wherefore things ordained by them as necessary to salvation have neither strength nor authority, unless it may be declared that they be taken out of holy Scripture.

Article xxi

How is the 21st Article of Religion relevant to twenty-first century Anglicans? With its reference to the 'commandment and will of princes', this Article may initially appear to some as something of a fossilised relic of the past, and unable to provide any reasonable application to dispersed groups of Anglicans around the world. Indeed, The Episcopal Church of the United States of America (TEC) omitted this Article in 1801 on the basis that it was 'partly of a local and civil nature.' This was, of course, a polite way of referring to the rejection of British rule following the American War of Independence!

Scripture and Church Councils

Nevertheless, this Article was highly relevant when initially published as part of the *Forty-Two Articles* (1553) and later the *Thirty-nine Articles* (1563). Pope Paul III had convoked the Council of Trent that ran from 1545 until 1563. This was highly irregular since the Holy Roman Emperor was traditionally supposed to have initiated councils of this magnitude. He had been supportive but struggled to garner the support of the French, who reluctantly attended and eventually refused to ratify the council's conclusions. Since the purpose of the council had been to counter the Reformation, the few invitations to Protestants only attracted a handful of Lutherans. Despite the irregular convocation and absence of Protestant and Eastern Christian communities, the council proclaimed itself a general and ecumenical council, and anathematised those who held (and presently hold) to reformed views of justification and the sacraments.

This was staggering stuff to the Reformers. General councils were best understood as those so-called ecumenical councils of the early church. They were ecumenical in the sense of reaching the world, just as the famous census of Augustus Caesar went out to the 'whole world' (*oikoumene*; Luke 2:1). They were ecumenical in the sense of rightly declaring Christian truth, just as the council of Jerusalem did as recorded in Acts 15. Thus, the *Reformatio Legum* (1552) and the Act of Supremacy (1558) accorded great honour and dignity to the first four councils: Nicaea I (325), Constantinople I (381), Ephesus I (431), and Chalcedon (451). Why then, did the homily 'Against the Peril of Idolatry' (1563) affirm two extra councils, Constantinople II (553) and Constantinople III (680-1)?

The clue to the answer lies embedded in this Article itself: the authority of the Scriptures over conciliar decisions. For, even the best of Christian councils are mere 'assemblies of men' whose sinful desires wage war against the 'Spirit and word of God' (Romans 8:5-13; cf. Article 9). Thus, the canons of councils are fallible and subject to error, whereas the sentences and sense of Scripture remain infallible and free of error. To argue otherwise, is to threaten the very necessity of the Scriptures according to Thomas Cranmer's former chaplain and theological advisor, Bishop John Ponet (1516-1556):

> If the church cannot err, and is a sufficient witness of the truth from time to time: then we have no need of the word written, but that we may be without: for all knowledge and ordering of doctrine remains in the church. (British Library, Add MS 89067, sig. f.47r.)

This is the reason for the selective approach to early ecumenical councils among early Anglicans. It also explains why Anglicans have chosen liberally from the canons of later 'so-called' ecumenical councils: the compulsory clerical celibacy of Lateran I (1123) was rejected, whereas the *filioque* doctrine of the Council of Florence (1439) was retained. The Reformation's wonderful rediscovery of the supremacy of the Holy Scriptures returned both the authority of the Church (Article 20) and the authority of General Councils (Article 21) to their proper places. Indeed, it was only because of the authority of Scripture that councils were granted their authority. As John Ponet continued:

> Christian people take not away the authority of such old fathers as agree in Christ's word, nor of such general councils as ground themselves thereupon but from such as forsake God's Word, walking by paths of men's traditions and inventions.

The Authority of Councils Today

Thus, we may draw five main lines of application for today.

First, we must face the fact that there is a great difference between early modern and current conceptions of 'princes.' The historical role of the 'prince' in ensuring the safe conduct and outcomes of church councils is now more or less redundant. At any rate, the Scriptures are silent concerning whether councils should be called by the likes of Emperors, Kings, or Presidents. Even if such a princely calling did obtain, it is unlikely that the various Christian communities would bend their authority structures to accommodate each other (e.g., the incompatibility of papal power with Eastern and Protestant denominations). Although nothing is impossible for God, the probability of another General Council seems fairly low at the present time.

Second, notwithstanding the above point, it is a good thing for Christian communities to gather 'to speak the truth in love' in councils and synods (Ephesians 4:15). We may not want to leave the intervals of our meetings as long as the Eastern churches (whose recent Pan-Orthodox council was the first in 1000 years), and there may be critical issues of discipline that need to be addressed. But the assembling of Christians for ecclesiastical and theological recalibration with Scripture is surely to be commended.

Third, the fallen reality described of General Councils remains the same for all synods and councils, be they diocesan, provincial, national, or transnational. We ought to be wary of hastily declaring synodical or conciliar decisions a 'movement of the Spirit', 'the mind of the Spirit', and so forth. It is only through careful and sustained reflection on the word of God that we may 'test the spirits' (1 John 4:1). Thus we should focus on the movement and the mind of the Scriptures.

Fourth, since the Scriptures ought to play the central role within the ecclesiastical and doctrinal decisions of synods and councils, then we must relativise all other sources of authority. Within certain debates (e.g., human sexuality) it may be tempting to preference modern science, sociology, or sentiment. But these are no substitute for the unchanging and unbreakable Scriptures. The dynamic of debates should be infused with the words of the Psalmist: 'Forever, O Lord, your word is firmly fixed in the heavens' (Psalm 119:80).

The Necessity of Scripture

Finally, we need to truly appreciate the necessity of the Scriptures. There are no creedal or canonical teachings that contain any saving truth found outside of the Scriptures. Indeed, the saving truths of conciliar creeds and canons only derive their force from the Scriptures. We must be absolutely clear: the church is not ultimately built on councils and synods, but 'on the foundation of the apostles and prophets, Christ Jesus himself being the cornerstone' (Ephesians 2:19).

Article 21 thus contains both ancient and contemporary significance. It may be tempting to wonder what might have happened to The Episcopal Church if it had retained this Article and its emphasis on the authority of Scripture over conciliar decisions. However, it is more important to look at ourselves and ask: do we truly appreciate the remarkable blessing of the Scriptures within God's plan of salvation?

The Revd Mark Earngey *is an Australian minister studying for a DPhil in Reformation history and theology at the University of Oxford.*

Questions for Reflection

1. How can the church councils you are familiar with (either local, regional, national, or international gatherings) be better 'governed with the Spirit and Word of God'?
2. If there was ever another worldwide ecumenical council, what should it discuss?
3. What role do you think the state should play in the church's decision making process?

Prayer

Almighty God, our heavenly Father, King of Kings and Lord of Lords: grant that we who are called by your holy word may give ourselves at once to obey all your commands, through the merits of your Son Jesus Christ, the shepherd and overseer of our souls. *Amen.*

BIBLE READING

Luke 23:39-43

One of the criminals who were hanged railed at him, saying, 'Are you not the Christ? Save yourself and us!' But the other rebuked him, saying, 'Do you not fear God, since you are under the same sentence of condemnation? And we indeed justly, for we are receiving the due reward of our deeds; but this man has done nothing wrong.' And he said, 'Jesus, remember me when you come into your kingdom.' And he said to him, 'Truly, I say to you, today you will be with me in paradise.'

STARTER QUESTION

Where did the criminal on the cross next to Jesus go when he died?

ARTICLE XXII

OF PURGATORY

The Romish Doctrine concerning Purgatory,
Pardons, Worshipping, and Adoration,
as well of Images as of Reliques, and also
invocation of Saints, is a fond thing vainly
invented, and grounded upon no warranty
of Scripture, but rather repugnant to the
Word of God.

ARTICLE XXII

D uring their Reformation, the leading English divines necessarily focussed a considerable effort on demonstrating the wrongness of several core beliefs of the late medieval Roman Catholic Church. Foremost among these were beliefs about salvation, authority in the church, and the afterlife—with the latter being the focus of Article 22.

THE ROMAN DOCTRINE OF THE AFTERLIFE

The 'Romish Doctrine' of the afterlife was quite complex and made up of a number of interrelated parts. First and perhaps foremost was *Purgatory*, the supposed antechamber of hell where the saved-but-not-yet-purified members of the church went upon their death in order to be 'purged' of the guilt or stain of their sin—a process that was torturously painful and which could last thousands upon thousands of years.

Second was *Pardons*, which were the remissions of that purgatorial pain as granted by the Catholic Church to those who either made certain financial donations (i.e. paid for them), or who completed various prescribed rituals to demonstrate their piety and submission.

Finally, *Worshipping and Adoration* of *Images* and *Relics*, and *Invocation of Saints* were all expressions of the cult of the saints, which was a pervasive part of late medieval English Catholicism.

This 'cult' was not an underground, deviant religious sub-group, like the cults of today, but rather a broad and general obsession with those departed believers who were believed to have avoided purgatory and instead been translated directly into heaven as reward for the great quality and purity of their mortal lives. These 'saints' were regularly idolised by the worship of their memory, and by the reverence shown to their pictures and relics which were believed to either contain, or channel, special grace. In some cases, the saints were even directly called upon to answer prayers.

Rejecting Rome's Inventions

Of course, all of this was completely unacceptable to the Protestant Reformers. Not only did they realise that these beliefs had facilitated the exercise of an enormous amount of power and control by the Roman Catholic Church over the peoples of Christendom, they also recognised that the entire Roman view of the afterlife was simply a 'fond thing, vainly invented, and grounded upon no warranty of Scripture, but rather repugnant to the Word of God.'

It was because of this that the Roman view of the afterlife was challenged from the very earliest days of the Reformation: Luther's *Ninety-Five Theses* of 1517 were mostly concerned with abuses of the Roman system of pardons. It is also worth noting that England's first significant movement away from the old Roman doctrine of purgatory came through its earliest Articles of Religion: the *Ten Articles* of 1536. Those Articles said of those who had died, 'forasmuch as the place where they be, the name thereof, and kind of pains there, also be to us uncertain by Scripture' and that it is only God 'to whom is known their estate and condition.' This is a remarkable declaration given that fifteen years earlier, Henry VIII had included a case for purgatory as the opening to his *Defence of the Seven Sacraments*, the work that won him the title Defender of the Faith from Pope Leo X.

Contrary to the views of the Roman Catholic Church, the Bible teaches that no one has any further penalty or punishment to pay for their sin once they accept the merits of Christ's death. Isaiah 53:4–6 makes plain that the Lord's servant has taken our punishment and made us whole; has healed us by his bruises. There is no sense in Scripture that Jesus' death was only a part-payment for sin, with the rest to be made up by the extreme suffering of his people between their own deaths and resurrection. Instead, Paul writes in 2 Corinthians 5:6–8 and Philippians 1:21–23 that if he were to die, that would only send him to a far better place—home with the Lord—which is exactly where we find the martyred believers in Revelation 6:9–11. And in 1 Thessalonians 4:13–18 he teaches that this is where believers remain waiting until they return with Jesus at his second coming.

This view of the intermediate state was standard amongst the mainstream Reformers and it is strongly argued for by John Calvin in *Psychopannychia*, his first theological work. It was also, in fact, quite explicit in Article 40 of the *Forty-Two Articles* of 1553, of which the *Thirty-Nine Articles* are a revision. Article 40 was directed against Soul Sleep and Conditionalism, which are the two forms of Christian Mortalism. The former is what Calvin wrote against, and is the belief that the soul is unconscious between death and resurrection. The latter is the view that the soul ceases to exist from death until it is made new again with the body. Once these two ideas are excluded along with purgatory, the only remaining possibility for believers is the biblical teaching of a conscious intermediate state between death and resurrection that is enjoyed in the very presence of Christ.

The Pastoral Significance of Biblical Doctrine

While it could be easy to push consideration of the intermediate state aside, as though it were a largely irrelevant theological obscurity, just a little reflection reveals how pastorally important truths concerning the afterlife are. When a dearly loved Christian sister or brother faces death or dies, we do not need to be uninformed regarding their fate. Instead, we can be deeply comforted with the great truths that they are now with Jesus, the object of all their deepest hopes and longings, and that they are safe and secure until the day of his return to earth when they will be present as he consummates his kingdom. We can most certainly be assured that they are not suffering the pains of purgatory which, in the last analysis, is only a cruel imaginary place. And in addition to our own comfort, being rid of Roman Catholic beliefs about the after-life frees us to direct all our praise and petition away from anyone and anything less than Christ himself—who is our only true and sure hope and intercessor.

The Revd Dr Tim Patrick *is the Principal of the Bible College of South Australia, an affiliated college of the Australian College of Theology.*

Questions for Reflection

1. Why is the biblical doctrine of the afterlife both a comfort and a challenge?
2. What is the biblical place of images in worship?
3. To whom does the Bible encourage us to pray?

Prayer

King of the ages, immortal, invisible, the only God, to whom all honour and glory are due: grant us grace to follow the virtuous and godly living of those who have died in Christ that we may come to those inexpressible joys that you have prepared for those who sincerely love you, through the merits of Jesus Christ our Lord. *Amen.*

BIBLE READING

Titus 1:5-9

This is why I left you in Crete, so that you might put what remained into order, and appoint elders in every town as I directed you—if anyone is above reproach, the husband of one wife, and his children are believers and not open to the charge of debauchery or insubordination. For an overseer, as God's steward, must be above reproach. He must not be arrogant or quick-tempered or a drunkard or violent or greedy for gain, but hospitable, a lover of good, self-controlled, upright, holy, and disciplined. He must hold firm to the trustworthy word as taught, so that he may be able to give instruction in sound doctrine and also to rebuke those who contradict it.

STARTER QUESTION

Can you summarise in 3 or 4 words the qualities of the people Titus was told he should appoint as overseers in the churches?

ARTICLE XXIII

OF MINISTERING IN THE CONGREGATION

~

It is not lawful for any man to take upon
him the office of publick preaching,
or ministering the Sacraments in the
Congregation, before he be lawfully called,
and sent to execute the same. And those
we ought to judge lawfully called and sent,
which be chosen and called to this work by
men who have publick authority given unto
them in the Congregation, to call and send
Ministers into the Lord's vineyard.

ARTICLE XXIII

Committed disciples of Jesus Christ will periodically ask themselves how they can best serve the Lord within his church. For a number, this question will take the particular form of asking whether or not they ought to set their sights on the ordained ministry. They will then, with the encouragement of senior church representatives, start wondering whether they have a 'vocation' or 'calling' for ordained ministry. If they believe they do, then they might wonder why the Church of England has such elaborate selection procedures. After all, if God has called them, why should Bishops' Advisers get in the way?

CALLING

Article 23 helps us to see this issue from a more biblical stand-point. The Bible has a number of things to say about a 'calling.' It stresses that the first and most fundamental calling is that of God who calls people to belong to his family (Romans 8:28-30). That same passage also tells us that once we have been adopted into his family, we are called to grow into the likeness of Christ.

However, when it comes to our role within the church, Article 23 reminds us that 'calling' is primarily something that congregations do towards particular individuals, through authorised representatives: 'And those we ought to judge lawfully called and sent, which be chosen and called to this work by men who have publick authority given unto them in the Congregation, to call and send Ministers into the Lord's vineyard.'

So although as we shall see, the subjective prompting of the Holy Spirit has a part to play in deciding on ordination, a calling is primarily from other people. Thus in Titus 1:5, Paul gives to Titus the responsibility of appointing elders in every town and is given the characteristics for which he should look. In 2 Timothy 2:2, Paul tells Timothy to 'entrust to faithful men' what he has heard from Paul, so that they can teach others also. Timothy himself only received his gift when, according to 1 Timothy 4:14, the 'council of elders laid their hands' on him. It seems therefore that 'selection' by others is the primary evidence of a calling to ordained ministry in an individual's life.

The Church of England therefore takes an entirely biblical approach in having a selection process for those who are going to be put forward for ordination training. The fact that the selection process can be long drawn out and therefore frustrating to some, should not lead us to deny its place in principle.

CRITERIA

What then should 'advisers' and ultimately bishops (i.e. those 'who have publick authority given unto them in the Congregation') be looking for in determining whether or not to call people into the ordained ministry?

Both Titus 1 and 1 Timothy 3 emphasise that godliness of character is primary. This is to be looked for both in their personal conduct and habits as well as in their family relationships. They are to be 'above reproach' and therefore have a good public reputation. What is more, they should not be recent converts (1 Timothy 3:6), lest they become 'puffed up.' These are such wise words since it is all too easy to fall in behind someone who is enthusiastic in their ministry, but whose lack of maturity has led them to glorify themselves rather than Christ.

There is an additional requirement for overseers/elders.

According to 1 Timothy 3:2, they must be 'able to teach.' Titus 1:9 puts it like this: 'He must hold firm to the trustworthy word as taught, so that he may be able to give instruction in sound doctrine and also to rebuke those who contradict it.' The primary job of the ordained minister is to teach God's word. This doesn't just mean standing up every Sunday and expounding Scripture. Teaching certainly involves preaching, but it also involves helping people discover truths from God's word for themselves; building loving relationships and showing care, so that the message we convey has credibility; and it is about having the courage and sensitivity to know how to put it into practice in church life—so that members of our congregations can see we are taking the Bible's teaching seriously.

Conviction

The traditional view of 'vocation' is that this is the result of someone combining a gift with a personal inclination to use that gift in their everyday work. So if the Bible tells us that 'gifts' have to be recognised by others, does it have anything to say about our personal inclination?

The answer is 'yes—but not much'! in 1 Corinthians 14:1 we read: 'Pursue love and earnestly desire the spiritual gifts, especially that you may prophesy'—the context being that one of these gifts is teaching. And in 1 Timothy 3:1, 'The saying is trustworthy: If anyone aspires to the office of overseer, he desires a noble task.'

The implication of these references is that individuals may expect to have an inner conviction, prompted by the Holy Spirit, that ordained ministry is the right avenue to pursue—but that on its own such a conviction does not yet amount to a calling. As Article 23 says: 'It is not lawful for any man to take upon him the office of publick preaching, or ministering the Sacraments in the Congregation, before he be lawfully called, and sent to execute the same.'

The Rt Revd Rod Thomas *is the Bishop of Maidstone.*

QUESTIONS FOR REFLECTION

1. What would happen if the people sent to lead churches were the opposite of those discussed in Titus 1:5-9?
2. Why would it be a bad idea to take such a position without being lawfully called and sent?
3. How should people be assessed and trained before being sent out as ministers?

PRAYER

God of grace, who calls all ministers both by their life and doctrine to set forth your true and living word: send out faithful workers into your harvest field, to teach others and share in suffering as good soldiers of our Lord Jesus, the chief Shepherd of the sheep, in whose name we pray. *Amen.*

Bible Reading

1 Corinthians 14:10-17

There are doubtless many different languages in the world, and none is without meaning, but if I do not know the meaning of the language, I will be a foreigner to the speaker and the speaker a foreigner to me. So with yourselves, since you are eager for manifestations of the Spirit, strive to excel in building up the church.

Therefore, one who speaks in a tongue should pray that he may interpret. For if I pray in a tongue, my spirit prays but my mind is unfruitful. What am I to do? I will pray with my spirit, but I will pray with my mind also; I will sing praise with my spirit, but I will sing with my mind also. Otherwise, if you give thanks with your spirit, how can anyone in the position of an outsider say 'Amen' to your thanksgiving when he does not know what you are saying? For you may be giving thanks well enough, but the other person is not being built up.

Starter Question

Why was the apostle Paul so keen that people should understand what was going on in the church meetings in Corinth?

ARTICLE XXIV

OF SPEAKING IN THE CONGREGATION IN SUCH A TONGUE AS THE PEOPLE UNDERSTANDETH

~

It is a thing plainly repugnant to the Word of God, and the custom of the Primitive Church, to have publick Prayer in the Church, or to minister the Sacraments in a tongue not understanded by the people.

ARTICLE XXIV

The use of vernacular language in our church services is something that we take for granted when attending church in our home country. In the medieval period, however, Latin was the language of the Church across Europe. This is not to say that English was never heard in church services. Most preaching to a lay audience was probably delivered in the vernacular. It was a requirement of canon law that a parish priest should be able to speak the language of his flock in order to minister to them. Moreover, by the fifteenth century, numerous devotional texts were available in English, at least to the wealthier and more educated sections of society.

MEDIEVAL INCOMPREHENSIBILITY

However, public prayers and the liturgy—notably surrounding the celebration of the Mass—remained in Latin. This did not mean that lay people were completely unable to participate in the service. They were encouraged to pray simple Latin prayers, such as the *Pater noster* or *Ave Maria*, during the Mass and to follow the service, changing posture at appropriate moments by kneeling, raising arms in adoration, and gazing up at the elevation of the Host, when the bread was believed to become the Body of Christ. However, the use of Latin meant that the doctrinal content of the Eucharist was shrouded in mystery and remained the preserve of a clerical elite. As one medieval historian has put it, 'participation was an act of faith, not comprehension.' (M. Aston, *Faith and Fire*)

Indeed, the incomprehensibility of the liturgy, particularly during the Mass, was seen as an integral part of its value as a sacred mystery, mediated through the priest. As the Roman Catholic medieval historian, Eamon Duffy, has explained in *The Stripping of the Altars*, 'It was part of the power of the words of consecration that they were hidden, too sacred to be communicated to the 'lewed' [*unlearned*], and this very element of mystery gave legitimacy to the sacred character of Latin itself, as higher and holier than the vernacular.'

Sacramental theology was not intended to be understood or even discussed by lay people; the terminology used to discuss it by theologians had no vernacular equivalent until Wycliffe's translation work in the late fourteenth century. As one fifteenth-century commentator, probably a Dominican friar, wrote, 'Many things are to be hidden and not shown to the people, lest being known and familiar they should be cheapened... The mysteries of the faith are not to be communicated to the simple.'

The church did make some attempts to provide religious education for the laity. The *Lay Folks Mass Book* was a late fourteenth-century rhyming manual, written in English, designed to take lay people step-by-step through the Mass. It did not offer a translation of the liturgy, however, but provided a series of allegorical meditations for each stage of the service. In fact, its author presented lack of comprehension as a benefit; it was, he claimed, similar to the effect of a charm upon snakes, having a positive effect on the hearer even though they did not understand it: 'Though ye vnderstonde hit nought, / Ye may wel wite that god hit wrought.' [*Although you do not understand it, you may be sure that God crafted it.*]

REFORMATION INTELLIGIBILITY

By contrast, the insistence of the reformers that the words of salvation should be accessible to all, in their own tongue, extended not just to the Bible but also to church services, a point enshrined in Article 24. The writer of the Second Book of Homilies elaborated on this in Homily 9, drawing an analogy with the apostle Paul's insistence in 1 Corinthians 14 that the gift of tongues should not be exercised in public worship without interpretation. As Paul wrote, 'So with yourselves, if with your tongue you utter speech that is not intelligible, how will anyone know what is said? For you will be speaking into the air ... Otherwise, if you give thanks with your spirit, how can anyone in the position of an outsider say 'Amen' to your thanksgiving when he does not know what you are saying? For you may be giving thanks well enough, but the other person is not being built up.' (1 Corinthians 14:9, 16-17). The writer applied the same principle to the use of Latin; what is said in a church service should be edifying to all, 'which cannot be, unless common prayers and administration of sacraments be in a tongue known to the people.'

CONTEMPORARY EDIFICATION

It is not the use of Latin which represents a barrier to a congregation's understanding in many churches today. Yet the biblical principles of intelligibility and edification as the hallmarks of fruitful corporate worship remain relevant. Article 24 should prompt us to ask challenging questions about our church services. Are our services accessible to believers of all levels of literacy, education, and learning ability? How many of our prayers and set forms of worship are comprehensible to the enquirer visiting church for the first time? Even when we move away from the liturgy to a more informal style of prayer, there is a danger that our language is jargon-filled and says more about our ecclesiastical tribe than it tells the outsider about the God we worship.

Article 24 also focuses our attention on the Lord's Supper. Do the liturgy, gestures, and actions chosen by the minister during the communion service illuminate the gospel truths to which the sacrament points? Or do they encourage ambiguity and misunderstanding about the nature of the sacraments? And is our theological training adequate to equip ordinands to know the difference, in contrast to the poorly educated medieval priests who may not have had much more understanding of the Latin liturgy than their parishioners?

Intelligibility is a great asset in a church service, but it is only a means to a greater end: edification. As the writer of the Homilies put it, 'when prayers or the administration of Sacraments shall be in a tongue unknown to the hearers, which of them shall be thereby stirred up to lift his mind to God?' There is little benefit to the body of Christ in any form of worship that—deliberately or accidentally—makes a virtue of obscurity.

Dr Andrea Ruddick *is a medieval historian, a member of the Church Society council, and a vicar's wife in Morden, in south-west London.*

QUESTIONS FOR REFLECTION

1. Are the services in your church accessible to believers of all levels of literacy, education, and learning ability?
2. How many of the prayers and set forms of worship in your church are comprehensible to the enquirer visiting church for the first time?
3. Does every element of your Sunday service seek to edify and build up those present?

PRAYER

Heavenly Father, who has graciously spoken to us in
your clear and living word: build us up in our most
holy faith, that we may be filled with a knowledge of
your will in all spiritual wisdom and understanding,
through Christ our Lord. *Amen.*

Bible Reading

1 Corinthians 10:1-5, 14-17

For I do not want you to be unaware, brothers, that our fathers were all under the cloud, and all passed through the sea, and all were baptized into Moses in the cloud and in the sea, and all ate the same spiritual food, and all drank the same spiritual drink. For they drank from the spiritual Rock that followed them, and the Rock was Christ. Nevertheless, with most of them God was not pleased, for they were overthrown in the wilderness…

Therefore, my beloved, flee from idolatry. I speak as to sensible people; judge for yourselves what I say. The cup of blessing that we bless, is it not a participation in the blood of Christ? The bread that we break, is it not a participation in the body of Christ? Because there is one bread, we who are many are one body, for we all partake of the one bread.

Starter Question

Why were the Israelites not pleasing to God in their wilderness wanderings if they had access to spiritual sacraments from God?

ARTICLE XXV

OF THE SACRAMENTS

~

Sacraments ordained of Christ be not
only badges or tokens of Christian men's
profession, but rather they be certain sure
witnesses, and effectual signs of grace, and
God's good will towards us, by the which he
doth work invisibly in us, and doth not only
quicken, but also strengthen and confirm our
Faith in him.

There are two Sacraments ordained of Christ
our Lord in the Gospel, that is to say, Baptism,
and the Supper of the Lord.

Those five commonly called Sacraments, that
is to say, Confirmation, Penance, Orders,
Matrimony, and extreme Unction, are not
to be counted for Sacraments of the Gospel,
being such as have grown partly of the corrupt
following of the Apostles, partly are states of

life allowed in the Scriptures; but yet have not like nature of Sacraments with Baptism, and the Lord's Supper, for that they have not any visible sign or ceremony ordained of God. The Sacraments were not ordained of Christ to be gazed upon, or to be carried about, but that we should duly use them. And in such only as worthily receive the same they have a wholesome effect or operation: but they that receive them unworthily purchase to themselves damnation, as Saint Paul saith.

ARTICLE XXV

This is another Article which shows the biblical and Protestant nature of our confession of faith. It contains warnings and explanations and although penned by Cranmer is not quite in the same order as originally planned. It begins a series of seven Articles looking at the sacraments.

USING AND RECEIVING SACRAMENTS

I well remember as a boy, in the then very Roman Catholic Republic of Ireland, watching a Corpus Christi procession through a town on a rainy day. Everyone but us knelt in the street as the monstrance went by. I would have too if I believed in transubstantiation but I did not. So I am grateful for and understand the warning that 'the Sacraments were not ordained of Christ to be gazed upon, or to be carried about, but that we should duly use them.'

The Sacraments 'ordained of Christ' then are to be 'duly used' and 'worthily received.' What does that mean? First, we must distinguish between those sacraments of the gospel ordained by Christ and other 'commonly (i.e. wrongly) called' sacraments which may or may not have a useful place in the Christian life (matrimony, orders, and confirmation certainly do).

Secondly, we are to rightly understand the nature of gospel sacraments. They are 'visible words' or visual aids to understand the gospel and the atoning work of Christ for us. They are extensions of the word preached, that visibly reinforce the proclaimed good news. Without the word preached they lose their meaning but in the context of hearing and believing the gospel they strengthen and encourage the Christian.

Baptism visibly reminds us in water that we need the cleansing and forgiveness of our sins, and that through the atoning sacrifice of Christ for us God has provided for our need, and brings to the believing heart a whole new life. The Lord's Supper reminds us of all that Christ's death accomplished for us, that we can never safely move away from the foot of the cross in wonder and worship as we seek to live the Christian life, and that we need his sustaining grace and help if we are to live for him as we ought.

Listen to Cranmer in his magisterial work on the Lord's Supper explaining this:

> These things before rehearsed are sufficient to prove, that the eating of Christ's flesh and drinking of his blood, is not to be understood simply and plainly, as the words do properly signify, that we do eat and drink him with our mouths; but it is a figurative speech spiritually to be understood, that we must deeply print and fruitfully believe in our hearts, that his flesh was crucified and his blood shed, for our redemption. And this our belief in him, is to eat his flesh and to drink his blood, although they be not present here with us, but be ascended into heaven.

And again:

> And every good and faithful Christian man feels in himself how he feeds of Christ, eating his flesh and drinking his blood. For he puts the whole hope and trust of his redemption and salvation in that only sacrifice, which Christ made upon the cross, having his body

there broken, and his blood there shed for the remission of his sins. And this great benefit of Christ, the faithful man earnestly considers in his mind, chews and digests it with the stomach of his heart, spiritually receiving Christ wholly into him, and giving again himself wholly unto Christ.

And this is the eating of Christ's flesh and drinking of his blood, the feeling whereof is to every man the feeling how he eats and drinks Christ, which no evil man nor member of the Devil can do.

The sacraments then are spiritual food for spiritual people. The Article adds St. Paul's warning that unworthily received (i.e. without belief and trust in Christ's substitutionary atoning death for us) they add to our condemnation.

STRENGTHENING FAITH

The sacraments are 'not only badges or tokens of Christian men's profession' (a view associated with the continental reformer Zwingli, but I think perhaps an inadequate explanation of his teaching). Rather, they are means of encouraging and strengthening the believer's faith generally, and particularly in times of difficulty, doubt, or despair. They are both 'certain sure witnesses' that proclaim the gospel promises to us in a concrete fashion, and also 'effectual signs of grace' to those who receive them with a believing heart.

Let me use a useful but inadequate analogy. My wedding ring means a great deal to me not because of its value in gold, but because it visibly and visually reminds me of the amazing fact that my wife loves me and has made promises to me that reflect that. The sacraments 'strengthen and confirm our Faith in him', because we bask in, feed on, and are blessed by the wonderful fact that, as St. Paul says, 'the Son of God loved me and gave himself for me' (Galatians 2:20).

Cranmer in his preferred words of administration in the 1552 service of Holy Communion beautifully expresses this profound and wonderful gospel theology: 'Take and eat this in remembrance that Christ died for thee, and feed on him in your heart by faith with thanksgiving.' What comfort and what joy!

To sum up then, as J. I. Packer says in his *Concise Theology*, 'As the preaching of the Word makes the Gospel audible, so the sacraments make it visible, and God stirs up faith by both means.'

The Rt Revd Wallace Benn *is the President of Church Society, a former Bishop of Lewes, and author of Remember Your Leaders: Principles and Priorities for Leaders from Hebrews 13.*

QUESTIONS FOR REFLECTION

1. Why does Jesus think we need the sacraments of baptism and the Lord's supper?
2. How is it possible for us today to misuse these things?
3. If salvation is by grace alone through faith alone, what does it mean to receive these things 'worthily'?

PRAYER

Heavenly Father, you have lovingly called us by your word and sacraments that we might perceive Christ with our ears, our eyes, and all our senses: strengthen and confirm us through these pledges of your love, that we might feed on him in our hearts by faith, in whose name we pray. *Amen.*

BIBLE READING

Matthew 23:1-7, 11-12

Then Jesus said to the crowds and to his disciples, 'The scribes and the Pharisees sit on Moses' seat, so do and observe whatever they tell you, but not the works they do. For they preach, but do not practice. They tie up heavy burdens, hard to bear, and lay them on people's shoulders, but they themselves are not willing to move them with their finger. They do all their deeds to be seen by others. For they make their phylacteries broad and their fringes long, and they love the place of honour at feasts and the best seats in the synagogues and greetings in the marketplaces and being called rabbi by others... The greatest among you shall be your servant. Whoever exalts himself will be humbled, and whoever humbles himself will be exalted.'

STARTER QUESTION

To what extent does the effectiveness of someone's ministry come from their own holiness and consistency?

ARTICLE XXVI

OF THE UNWORTHINESS OF THE MINISTERS, WHICH HINDERS NOT THE EFFECT OF THE SACRAMENT

~

Although in the visible Church the evil be ever mingled with the good, and sometimes the evil have chief authority in the Ministration of the Word and Sacraments, yet forasmuch as they do not the same in their own name, but in Christ's, and do minister by his commission and authority, we may use their Ministry, both in hearing the Word of God, and in receiving of the Sacraments. Neither is the effect of Christ's ordinance taken away by their wickedness, nor the grace of God's gifts diminished from such as

by faith and rightly do receive the
Sacraments ministered unto them;
which be effectual, because of Christ's
institution and promise, although they
be ministered by evil men.
Nevertheless, it appertaineth to the
discipline of the Church, that inquiry
be made of evil Ministers, and that
they be accused by those that have
knowledge of their offences; and finally
being found guilty, by just judgement
be deposed.

ARTICLE XXVI

I t is not often that we find liberal Anglicans quoting from the Thirty-nine Articles. Nevertheless Article 26 is a favourite with some who want to say that evangelical ministers and their congregations should accept whatever bishop they are given and not raise questions about their teaching. Their argument is that the title of this Article states that unworthy ministers do not hinder the effect of any Sacrament they administer. Therefore evangelicals should accept the bishop they are given. Yet the logical conclusion of that would be that a professed Buddhist could administer Christian sacraments without any problem. That would seem bizarre and shows why it is important to understand the proper significance of this Article.

DONATISM

The background to the Article lies in the error of Donatism (not a heresy as some loosely say) which was an issue in the early centuries of the church in North Africa. This error can be found in any context in which there is misguided zeal for the purity of the church. It is about majoring over minors and breaking fellowship with faithful Christians. The error creates divisions between Christians. The great Augustine of Hippo saw that the resolution of the issue came about through recognising that the professing church will be a mixed body containing open sinners.

At the time of the Reformation, godly Christians understandably became very upset by what Griffith Thomas calls 'the gross lives of many of the Roman priests.' Their disgust meant that many were unwisely tempted to accept the arguments of Anabaptists who said that Christians should be baptised only by a godly minister. The first part of the Article addresses this issue and comes into our Thirty-nine Articles via Luther and then Cranmer. It states a principle that faithful Christians need to recognise. Jesus rebuked his disciples for a version of the Donatist spirit in Mark 9:38-41. The apostle John reminds us of how love for fellow Christians is diagnostic of real Christianity in 1 John 3-4. The apostle Paul warns us of the need to welcome a repentant offender in 2 Corinthians 1:7.

DISCIPLINE

However having noted the principle in the first part of Article 26 it is very important to note that its last paragraph was deliberately added in by Cranmer. In this, Cranmer recognises that the Donatist error is likely to arise when the Church does not take seriously its responsibility to exercise discipline on what he terms here 'Evil Ministers.'

And this of course is exactly the issue we face in many parts of the Church of England today. Donatism was a misguided attempt to preserve the purity of the Christian community. It is a wrong response to a serious problem. However we must note that both the Donatists and Augustine would have urged the necessity of separation from Pelagian or Arian heretics. In case we misunderstand Augustine, we should know that he is quoted as saying 'Neither must we subscribe to (i.e. obey) catholic bishops if they chance to err, or determine anything contrary to the canonical divine Scriptures' (*On the Unity of the Church*, 28).

This concern for discipline in the last part of Article 26 reflects biblical concerns that are found in the pastoral epistles and in Paul's teaching about breaking fellowship in 1 Corinthians 5:9-

11. And of course the same concern is found in the Ordinal where priests (presbyters) are to 'banish and drive away all erroneous and strange doctrines contrary to God's word.' Furthermore the collect for consecrating a Bishop refers specifically to the responsibility to administer godly discipline.

APPLYING THE ARTICLE TODAY

The point then of Article 26 is that it warns us not to make the error which the Donatists fell into in responding to ungodly behaviour in the professing church. But it also underlines the responsibility of church leaders to deal with ungodly ministers.

If in current circumstances you refuse to share fellowship with unfaithful congregation members or leaders who profess to be Christians, then you are exercising a discipline that has failed to be enforced by those who should. You are not a Donatist.

Indeed, those who so readily accuse biblical Christians of Donatism should reflect on how they themselves treat any who disagree with them on biblical grounds. If the impact of their position is that they exclude godly Christians from the fellowship of the Church then it is they who should be accused of Donatism. Article 20 warns against the Church ordaining something contrary to God's word written. When a conscience that is seeking to submit to the authority of Scripture cannot be accommodated within the Church then the consequences will be very grave.

What then should we do if we face a situation when we have to work out how to respond to a church leader who by their behaviour or by their teaching causes scandal and confusion to those who are sincerely seeking to submit to Christ and his word? The first thing is to remember what the first part of this Article 26 states. Be careful about misguided attempts to preserve the purity of the church. Sometimes ministers today receive requests for re-baptism which are often an expression of the idea that someone's first baptism was 'no good.' We should not be in the business of re-baptising. The consecration of women bishops has also made evangelical Christians think carefully about how they respond to the charge that they are only interested in having the bishops they want. We must avoid the spirit of Donatism.

However, in the face of an unfaithful church leader it is important to take the step of asking the appropriate authorities to exercise the discipline that the last part of the Article demands. If that responsibility which the Ordinal expects is not discharged then we will have no option but to express the break in fellowship in appropriate ways ourselves. You are never guilty of the Donatist error if you seek wise and godly discipline for those guilty of heresy.

The Revd Dr Mark Burkill *is the Vicar of Christ Church, Leyton, Chairman of the Latimer Trust, and author of* Unworthy Ministers: Donatism and Discipline Today.

Questions for Reflection

1. How should we feel about the fact that 'the evil be ever mingled with the good' in the church?
2. Is it wrong to take communion from a minister who does not seem to practice what he preaches?
3. What is the most appropriate way to seek discipline for those who seem to be 'evil ministers'?

Prayer

Risen and ascended Lord Jesus, you have given pastors and teachers as a gift to your church, to equip the saints for works of ministry: grant to all bishops, presbyters, and deacons faithful diligence so to teach your word and frame their lives that they may banish false opinions and be wholesome examples and patterns to the church for which you died. *Amen.*

BIBLE READING

Romans 6:3-8, 11

Do you not know that all of us who have been baptised into Christ Jesus were baptised into his death? We were buried therefore with him by baptism into death, in order that, just as Christ was raised from the dead by the glory of the Father, we too might walk in newness of life. For if we have been united with him in a death like his, we shall certainly be united with him in a resurrection like his. We know that our old self was crucified with him in order that the body of sin might be brought to nothing, so that we would no longer be enslaved to sin. For one who has died has been set free from sin. Now if we have died with Christ, we believe that we will also live with him... So you also must consider yourselves dead to sin and alive to God in Christ Jesus.

STARTER QUESTION

What is baptism all about according to the apostle Paul here?

Article XXVII

OF BAPTISM

~

Baptism is not only a sign of profession, and mark of difference, whereby Christian men are discerned from others that be not christened, but it is also a sign of Regeneration or new Birth, whereby, as by an instrument, they that receive Baptism rightly are grafted into the Church; the promises of the forgiveness of sin, and of our adoption to be the sons of God by the Holy Ghost, are visibly signed and sealed; Faith is confirmed, and Grace increased by virtue of prayer unto God. The Baptism of young Children is in any wise to be retained in the Church, as most agreeable with the institution of Christ.

ARTICLE XXVII

The last recorded words of our Lord in Matthew's Gospel were to his eleven disciples to go and make other disciples, baptising them in the name of the Father, and of the Son, and of the Holy Spirit, teaching them to observe all that Jesus had commanded (Matthew 28:19-20). The background to this command was the making and baptising of disciples that was part of Jesus' earthly ministry, as it had been part of John's (John 4:1-2). The combination of making disciples and the use of water baptism as a 'seal' or 'mark' of discipleship is striking.

The prophets of the Old Testament would call rebellious Israel back to God with a reminder of the covenant of circumcision. 'Circumcise yourselves to the Lord, remove the foreskin of your hearts' (Jeremiah 4:4; 6:10; 9:25f; cf. Deuteronomy 10:16). However, the last Old Testament prophet was John, God's messenger sent to prepare the way for the Lord's coming, so a new sign was required. More was needed than merely a reminder of their circumcision; a washing of water was needed, as a sign and seal of their sins having been washed away. The 'messenger of the covenant' was introducing something new, and the sign of that newness was water baptism, such that the distinction between the righteous and the wicked might once again be manifest (Malachi 3:1, 18).

Thus when Peter preached his sermon on the Day of Pentecost, his hearers asked what should they do. Peter's reply was clear: 'Repent and be baptised every one of you in the name of the Lord Jesus for the forgiveness of sins' (Acts 2:38). Likewise Paul's preaching of faith in Christ was invariably accompanied with the baptism of Christ's new disciples (Acts 16:31ff; 19:4f), just as he had been so baptised (Acts 9:18).

An Effective Sign

Article 27 first speaks of baptism as a sign of profession and mark of difference for Christians. This was not disputed in the sixteenth century and accords with both our Lord's and his apostles' teaching and practice. However, the Article then proceeds to assert that baptism is *more* than a sign of profession, it is also a sign of regeneration or new birth. Moreover, it is an effective sign ('as by an instrument'), such that those who receive it 'rightly are grafted into the Church.' This was to counter those who thought baptism was a *mere* sign of human response, many of whom also rejected the baptism of infants.

Baptism, rightly administered, is God's sign of his inclusion of the person so baptised into the fellowship of his church. It represents God's activity in changing the heart of the individual, a regeneration of the Holy Spirit, or in Jesus' words, being 'born of the Spirit' (John 4:8). It is no accident that baptism is a passive sacrament, unlike the Lord's Supper, where the participant is active ('take and eat'). One does not baptise oneself, one is baptised by another. Such 'passivity' extols the very grace of God in his prior working in the human heart which elicits the response of faith. For this reason Paul reminds his reader: 'God saved us, not because of deeds done by us in righteousness, but in virtue of his own mercy, by the washing of regeneration and renewal of the Holy Spirit' (Titus 3:5; cf. Ephesians 5:26; Hebrews 10:22).

Rightly Receiving Baptism

Baptism had been abused in the Medieval Church as a talisman or charm, such that those who were baptised considered themselves immune from God's judgment. Article 27, by contrast, speaks of the right reception of the sacrament—'they that receive Baptism rightly are grafted into the Church.' In other words it is not an 'automatically' effective sign, anymore than circumcision was an 'automatically' effective sign of salvation for Israel. The circumcision of the heart was needed; yet the circumcision of the flesh was the sign of such internal circumcision (Romans 2:29). That Paul compares the inner meaning of circumcision ('circumcision made without hands') with the reality of his hearers' own transition from death to life in the language of baptism is instructive (Colossians 2:11-12). This is primarily the work of God in our lives, and the rightful use of baptism enables faith to be 'confirmed, and grace increased by virtue of prayer unto God.' Whenever we witness a baptism, we are reminded of our own baptism, of God's promises to us, and so our own faith is strengthened and grace increased.

INFANT BAPTISM

The final sentence of the Article reminds us that the baptism of young children should be retained, as it is most agreeable with the institution of Christ. In contrast to the Anabaptists, the Reformers saw infant baptism as part of Christ's mandate 'to make disciples of all nations.' While it is often claimed that there is no example of infants being baptised in the New Testament, thoughtful readers of the Bible will recognise that Paul has no difficulty in describing 'all' of Israel as being baptised into Moses in the cloud and in the sea—infants as well as adults (1 Corinthians 10:2). This would be very misleading language if the apostle considered infants should not be baptised under the new covenant. Indeed, in the same letter, Paul describes the children of even one believer as 'holy', as opposed to 'unclean' (1 Corinthians 7:14).

The promise of God is to us *and* to our children (Genesis 17:7; Isaiah 59:20-21; Acts 2:39). They are not in a neutral zone awaiting salvation. They are the Lord's children. Not bramble bushes waiting to be grafted into the vine, but olive shoots around the table (Psalm 128:3). As surely as Paul's letter is addressed to the 'saints' at Ephesus, so he includes the children of believers within the same salutation (Ephesians 6:1).

It is inconceivable that the new covenant would be less inclusive than the old—quite the contrary. The expansion of God's salvation to include Jews and Gentiles does not at the same time become more restrictive within the family. That John the Baptist would call upon people to repent and be baptised, lest they come under God's judgment, suggests no believing Jewish parent would have left their children on the bank to receive God's wrath, but would have brought them forward to be baptised. Like Joshua, they too would have declared: 'As for me and my house we will serve the Lord!' (Joshua 24:15).

The Most Revd Dr Glenn N Davies *is the Archbishop of Sydney.*

QUESTIONS FOR REFLECTION

1. Of what is baptism a sign?
2. How can baptism be rightly or wrongly received?
3. On what grounds can the children of believers be baptised?

PRAYER

Almighty God, into the death of whose Son we have
been baptised, that we might die to sin and live for
righteousness: make us steadfast in faith, joyful in
hope, and rooted in love so that united with him we
may pass through the waves of this troublesome world
and finally come to the land of everlasting life, through
Jesus Christ our Lord. *Amen.*

BIBLE READING

Matthew 26:26-30

Now as they were eating, Jesus took bread, and after blessing it broke it and gave it to the disciples, and said, 'Take, eat; this is my body.' And he took a cup, and when he had given thanks he gave it to them, saying, 'Drink of it, all of you, for this is my blood of the covenant, which is poured out for many for the forgiveness of sins. I tell you I will not drink again of this fruit of the vine until that day when I drink it new with you in my Father's kingdom.' And when they had sung a hymn, they went out to the Mount of Olives.

STARTER QUESTION

What did Jesus tell his disciples to do with the bread and wine?

ARTICLE XXVIII

OF THE LORD'S SUPPER

~

The Supper of the Lord is not only a
sign of the love that Christians ought
to have among themselves one to
another; but rather is a Sacrament of
our Redemption by Christ's death:
insomuch that to such as rightly,
worthily, and with faith, receive the
same, the Bread which we break is
a partaking of the Body of Christ;
and likewise the Cup of Blessing is a
partaking of the Blood of Christ.
Transubstantiation (or the change
of the substance of Bread and
Wine) in the Supper of the Lord,
cannot be proved by holy Writ; but
is repugnant to the plain words of
Scripture, overthroweth the nature of a

Sacrament, and hath given occasion to many superstitions.

The Body of Christ is given, taken, and eaten, in the Supper, only after an heavenly and spiritual manner. And the mean whereby the Body of Christ is received and eaten in the Supper is Faith.

The Sacrament of the Lord's Supper was not by Christ's ordinance reserved, carried about, lifted up, or worshipped.

ARTICLE XXVIII

We live by faith and not by sight. This, as most of us know, can be hard. Christ, the one we trust, the object of our faith, is not physically with us. We can't see him or touch him. Can we really be sure he loves us? Is our future with him really secure? We find ourselves crying out to Jesus like the man in Mark 9:24—'I believe; help my unbelief!' We have his word to hold onto, his gospel promises. But does he give us anything else?

He does, and Article 28 is here to protect it. This Article is a masterpiece of careful, concise, pastorally-motivated Reformed theology. And its main purpose seems to be to protect from neglect or abuse one of the means Jesus has graciously given us to overcome our unbelief. Jesus has given us what we call the Lord's Supper or Holy Communion—for our encouragement, assurance, and perseverance in faith.

THE SUPPER AS A SACRAMENT

The Article protects Jesus' purposes for the Supper in two main ways. The first is to help us think about the Supper rightly as a *sacrament*. The word 'sacrament' will perhaps seem a little obscure or unhelpfully religious to some ears, but Article 25 has already helpfully explained that (rightly understood) sacraments are good things: gifts of God to the church, 'effectual signs of grace and

God's good will towards us.' They are means through which God can work to 'quicken' (that is, stimulate), strengthen, and confirm our faith. This is a fairly standard Reformed understanding of a sacrament.

Applied to the Lord's Supper, the visible—and edible!—signs of the bread and wine point us to Christ, and our redemption by his death. But these are powerful signposts. They are 'effectual.' To the Christian taking the bread and wine rightly, worthily and with faith, receiving the sign is nothing less than a 'partaking' of Christ, feeding on him and what he has done for us.

Now, the Article goes on to clarify that this feeding is 'in a heavenly and spiritual manner'; it is not physical. Nonetheless, if received and eaten with faith, the Supper does in a 'spiritual manner' connect us to Christ and what he has done, and will be effective in evoking more faith and assurance.

The Supper works in a believer very much like the written or spoken word of the gospel. Like the written or spoken word, it points us to Christ and brings about faith. If received with faith, it generates more faith. Like the written or spoken gospel word, it proclaims Christ's death (1 Corinthians 11:26). Indeed, the connection between the Supper and the written or spoken gospel word is essential (which is why the Communion Service in the Book of Common Prayer insists that a sermon should always be preached).

The Supper is also *distinct* from the word received visually or aurally, in that it's received through tasting, eating, and drinking. It thus expands the ways in which we encounter and connect by faith with Christ and the truth of the gospel, bringing about a deeper remembrance, faith, and assurance. Jesus commands us, '*Do this* [tasting, eating, and drinking] in remembrance of me' (Luke 22:19; 1 Corinthians 11:24–25). He doesn't merely command, 'Remember me.'

The Supper is therefore much more than a celebration of our love for one another. Article 28 also corrects those who might neglect the Supper, or who treat it superficially in other ways. To do so would be to short-change one another of a God-given means of strengthening our remembrance of Christ and his death for us.

THE SUPPER AND CHRIST

The second way Article 28 protects Jesus' purposes for the Supper is to insist upon an orthodox understanding of its underlying Christology. By 'orthodox Christology', I mean that the one Lord Jesus Christ is both fully God and fully human. It's in this true Christ that we place our trust for salvation and find assurance— because, as a man, he took on human flesh, and then bore *our* sins and *our* death in his *human* body on the cross. It matters hugely therefore that he is indeed fully human, and our Reformers rightly insisted that to be fully human means being in just one physical location at any one time. The rubric at the end of the Communion Service in the Book of Common Prayer puts it like this:

> ...the natural Body and Blood of our Saviour Christ are in Heaven, and not here; it being against the truth of Christ's natural body to be at one time in more places than one.

Quite so.

To suggest that the bread and wine somehow 'become' the physical human body and blood of Christ—as in the doctrine of transubstantiation and some related views—is not only nonsensical but teaches a false, heterodox Christology. It is, the Article claims, 'repugnant to the plain words of Scripture' (especially those supporting the humanity of Christ or describing the Last Supper, when Jesus's physical body and blood remained physically separate and distinct from the bread and wine). What's more, it 'overthrows the nature of a sacrament', as the false Christology robs the Christian of the assurance of salvation the Supper was supposed to strengthen.

The Supper and Superstitions

Even more than this, when the Supper is distorted by suggesting any kind of 'change of substance' in the bread and wine, it 'has given rise to many superstitions.' It opens up the temptation to treat created things as divine things to be adored—which, as the Communion Service rubric reminds us, is *idolatry*, 'to be abhorred of all faithful Christians.' Examples include those mentioned at the end of the Article: when the bread or wine are 'reserved, carried about, lifted up, or worshipped.' If such activities sound perversely weird, that's because they are.

J.C. Ryle says this about Article 28 in his book *Knots Untied* (in chapter 8, on the Lord's Supper):

> I shall make no remark on these words. I only ask plain churchmen to put them side by side with High Church statements about the Lord's Supper, and to observe the utter contrariety that exists between them. I appeal to the common sense of all impartial and unprejudiced Englishmen.

Many of us will have thought similar things when confronted with actual practice in ostensibly Anglican Communion Services, shuddering as we recall the plain words of Article 28—rendered speechless by the utter contrariety between its words and what we're seeing. Likewise when it comes to suffering the lazy theological ineptitude of some of the Eucharistic Prayers in *Common Worship*.

Are we being too sensitive, or too contentious if we complain? Well, maybe, if our only concern were to win an argument. On the other hand if we are driven by the same pastoral concern that underlies Article 28, then should we not be similarly horrified when Christian brothers and sisters are robbed of assurance or led astray into idolatry? Why would we want to obscure or distort the Supper? It is after all a precious component of Jesus' loving response to us whenever we cry out, 'I believe; help my unbelief!'

The Revd Dr Ben Cooper *is Minister for Training at Christ Church Fulwood in Sheffield and the author of* Positive Complementarianism: The key biblical texts.

Questions for Reflection

1. Why is it important to remember that Jesus's physical body is in heaven until he comes again?
2. How can the Supper be rightly or wrongly used?
3. How does the Lord's Supper strengthen our faith in Jesus?

Prayer

Almighty God, whose Son Jesus Christ suffered death upon the cross for our redemption, and is seated at your right hand in heaven until he comes again in glory to judge the living and the dead: grant that by faith in his blood we and your whole church may obtain forgiveness of our sins and share every spiritual blessing in him, who reigns with you and the Holy Spirit, one God, now and forever. *Amen.*

BIBLE READING

1 Corinthians 11:23-29

For I received from the Lord what I also delivered to you, that the Lord Jesus on the night when he was betrayed took bread, and when he had given thanks, he broke it, and said, 'This is my body, which is for you. Do this in remembrance of me.' In the same way also he took the cup, after supper, saying, 'This cup is the new covenant in my blood. Do this, as often as you drink it, in remembrance of me.' For as often as you eat this bread and drink the cup, you proclaim the Lord's death until he comes.

Whoever, therefore, eats the bread or drinks the cup of the Lord in an unworthy manner will be guilty concerning the body and blood of the Lord. Let a person examine himself, then, and so eat of the bread and drink of the cup. For anyone who eats and drinks without discerning the body eats and drinks judgment on himself.

STARTER QUESTION

How can taking the Lord's Supper be a dangerous thing to do?

ARTICLE XXIX

OF THE WICKED WHICH EAT NOT THE BODY OF CHRIST IN THE USE OF THE LORD'S SUPPER

~

The Wicked, and such as be void of a lively faith, although they do carnally and visibly press with their teeth (as Saint Augustine saith) the Sacrament of the Body and Blood of Christ, yet in no wise are they partakers of Christ: but rather, to their condemnation, do eat and drink the sign or Sacrament of so great a thing.

Article XXIX

Sometimes it is only when you sit down and do a worked example that you understand a truth thoroughly. When I was 15 my local Roman Catholic priest asked me to choose whether to be a Roman Catholic or an Anglican. As we discussed Scripture and salvation the worked example of just one person, Mary the mother of Jesus, was very helpful to me. If she was sinless then I should be a Catholic; if she was sinful like everybody else then I should be a Protestant.

The example of 'the wicked... in the use of the Lord's Supper' does the same job with the sacraments. What happens when an unbeliever, or someone living in unrepentant sin, takes the bread and eats it? They certainly 'carnally and visibly press with their teeth' a piece of bread. Sometimes when you're taking a service you fear for their dentures because of how visibly they press. But is anything else happening as well? If they also receive the true body of Christ then something physical happened to the bread and wine before it got to their teeth. If they don't, then the bread is still bread, and the real partaking only happens spiritually and by faith.

This truth was fully explained in Article 25, 'in such only as worthily receive the same they have a wholesome effect or operation', and Article 28 'the Body of Christ is... eaten... only after an heavenly and spiritual manner.' But the worked example was so controversial that it is one of only two Articles that need a reassuring quote from an Ancient Church Father (Augustine's *Homilies on the Gospel of John*, Tractate 26.18 on John 6:41-59). It was also the only Article approved by the clergy in 1563 that the government kept out until 1571. For that first, nervous decade of Elizabeth's reign it was not politically possible to be this clear, and the Church of England only had 38 Articles.

The Intention of this Article

That political context means we are able to be certain about the intention of this Article. It clinches the denial of the Roman Catholic doctrine of Transubstantiation, and by 1570 Elizabeth had been excommunicated for a year so there was nothing to lose with the Pope, but that isn't really the purpose of Article 29. Article 28 was already offensive enough to the Pope.

Article 29 was kept out to leave vague the relationship between Anglicanism and Lutheranism; and it was put back in to make clear that Anglicans do not believe the Lutheran doctrine of the Real Presence. In 1577 the Lutheran Formula of Concord made that clarity mutual and anathematised anyone who believed the doctrine of Article 29. Historians think that Elizabeth spent the 1560s hoping for an alliance with the Lutheran princes, but by 1571 was prepared to choose doctrinal clarity over political hopes. (Stephen Hampton has a very helpful chapter in Anthony Milton's new *Oxford History of Anglicanism: Volume I* which gives much more detail.)

Article 29, then, is for anyone who wants to understand clearly the Anglican doctrine of the Lord's Supper. We are certainly not somewhere halfway between Roman Catholicism and Protestantism. In fact, we are not even somewhere halfway between Luther and Calvin. Article 29 unambiguously commits the Church of England to the Reformed understanding when it comes to the sacraments, and unambiguously denies the Lutheran understanding.

Practical Applications

Reflecting on this Article has helped me in two practical ways. First, many of us rejoice that we have many unbelievers who come to our churches. We work hard to make them welcome, and we hope that, over time, they may come to believe the gospel they are hearing. Article 29 makes clear that we are not doing them any good by giving them communion.

Augustine, in his sermon on John 6, points us to the examples of rebellious Israel in the desert, Judas, and the crowd of 5000 fed by Jesus, to prove his point that pressing with your teeth only does harm. All three examples are serious warnings, and fit with 1 Corinthians 11:29 as quoted by Article 25. This is important when much evangelism among Catholic Anglicans is based around Communion services, and when many Evangelicals are attracted to Catholic models of evangelism.

Second, this Article provides an opportunity to think again about our own reception of the bread and wine. It is very easy to think too much in physical, carnal terms about what is happening. It is also easy to receive as if the benefits were automatic, and grounded in the religious ceremony that has just happened, rather than in what is happening inside you. Augustine encouraged his congregation to think about our desire, our faith, and our heart not about our tongues, our teeth, and our tummies. Are we spiritually hungry? Are we trusting in Jesus and his death once for all? Are we repentant of our sins?

Those are the truths, and the spiritual habits that this Article defends. Sometimes the worked example is crucial for really living by the truths we believe.

The Revd Charlie Skrine *is Associate Rector St. Helen's, Bishopsgate and a member of the General Synod of the Church of England.*

QUESTIONS FOR REFLECTION

1. Why would it be loving to warn unbelievers not to take the Lord's Supper?
2. What should we think about when we take, eat, and drink the Supper?
3. Why is it important that this Article quotes St Augustine?

PRAYER

Almighty God, whose only Son Jesus Christ was crucified for us and for our salvation: grant that we may so feed on him in our hearts with a lively faith that we may evermore dwell in him and he in us, in whose name we pray. *Amen.*

Bible Reading

Hebrews 9:11-15

But when Christ appeared as a high priest of the good things that have come, then through the greater and more perfect tent (not made with hands, that is, not of this creation) he entered once for all into the holy places, not by means of the blood of goats and calves but by means of his own blood, thus securing an eternal redemption. For if the blood of goats and bulls, and the sprinkling of defiled persons with the ashes of a heifer, sanctify for the purification of the flesh, how much more will the blood of Christ, who through the eternal Spirit offered himself without blemish to God, purify our conscience from dead works to serve the living God. Therefore he is the mediator of a new covenant, so that those who are called may receive the promised eternal inheritance, since a death has occurred that redeems them from the transgressions committed under the first covenant.

Starter Question

What is so important about the blood of Christ?

ARTICLE XXX

OF BOTH KINDS

The Cup of the Lord is not to be denied to
the Lay-people; for both the parts of the
Lord's Sacrament, by Christ's ordinance and
commandment, ought to be ministered to
all Christian men alike.

Article xxx

Article 30 is the third Article relating to the Lord's Supper. Article 28 denies the Roman Catholic doctrine of transubstantiation (where the elements of bread and wine become the body and blood of Jesus), insisting that the elements are signs pointing back to Christ, not Christ himself. Article 29 argues that those without faith who partake in the Lord's Supper are not partaking in Christ, and in fact are bringing condemnation on themselves.

Article 30 gives instructions of how the Lord's Supper is to be given or administered to the congregation. It declares that both elements, and in particular the cup, are to be served to all Christian members of the congregation. To our minds this may seem a strange instruction, as it might never have occurred to us that when we come to the Lord's Supper we might only be offered the bread and not the cup. That's certainly true for me.

Medieval Reservations about the Cup

So why did the Reformers feel the need to insist on this? After all when Jesus established what we've come to call the Lord's Supper on the night before he died, he clearly invited the disciples to eat the bread and drink the cup in remembrance of him (Matthew 26:26-30; Luke 22:19-22). In the early church the practice of serving both the bread and wine continued. For example in

1 Corinthians 11 as Paul instructs the church about the correct manner in which they were to come to celebrate the Lord's Supper, it's clear the expectation was that people would be eating the bread and drinking from the cup, linking the practice of the Corinthians to the night before Jesus' death (1 Corinthians 11:23-27).

Yet by the time of the medieval church, the situation had changed. No longer was the cup offered to members of the congregation, instead it was reserved for the presiding priest. There are several theories about how this practice emerged, though it is not entirely clear. One possibility is that due to issues around hygiene it was not right to drink from a common cup. Another is that the elements were to be so revered that they were to be kept from human contamination. Bread was placed straight on the tongue of the recipient and the wine was withheld from 'the common people.'

The theology which was developed to justify giving communion in only one kind was this: because bodies have blood in them, giving only the body of Jesus meant that in reality people were in fact being given both body and blood! They did not need the cup, and as the priest was the representative of the people before God he would take the cup for them. This simply reinforced the notion of the priest as somewhat separate from the rest of the congregation and as a mediator between God and the people.

There were some rumblings against this practice in the fifteenth century when the Hussites of Bohemia broke with the tradition of Rome and began to administer the communion in 'both kinds' in their congregations. Their practice was condemned at the Council of Constance in 1415. Their leader, Jan Huss, was burned at the stake for what the council considered heresy.

The final session of the Council of Trent, the counter-reformation council, held in the 1560's confirmed the Decree of the Constance Council and determined that:

> Wherefore, holy Mother Church, knowing this her authority in the administration of the sacraments, al-

though the use of both species has, from the beginning of the Christian religion, not been unfrequent, yet, in progress of time, that custom having been already very widely changed, she, induced by weighty and just reasons, has approved of this custom of communicating under one species, and decreed that it was to be held as a law; which it is not lawful to reprobate, or to change at pleasure, without the authority of the Church itself' (Session 21, Chapter 2, 1562).

The historical account of the practice in some ways only adds to the strangeness of this Article. In one sense it seems like a fairly minor if not pedantic issue. Yet, theologically, for the Reformers it was important. At the heart of this Article are two important doctrines.

REFORMATION INSISTENCE ON DRINKING THE WINE

First, the Roman practice implied there was another mediator between God and humanity, alongside Christ. This notion was repugnant to the Reformers (see Hebrews 9:11-15). By withholding the cup from the congregation and taking the wine himself, the priest was in fact standing in their place.

Which leads to the second important theological truth: The Reformers' conviction about the priesthood of all believers (cf. 1 Peter 2:5). This view holds that the church is a company of priests who bring to God 'a sacrifice of praise' (Hebrews 13:15), and therefore there isn't one person who stands in place of the congregation representing them to God. We all have access to God equally.

Today the practice of receiving the communion in both kinds has become more commonplace in the Roman Catholic Church, though it is not universal. It is important to protect the practice of giving the communion in both kinds for two significant reasons. Biblically, as the Article suggests, it continues the tradition in the way Christ ordained and commanded, and in line with the early church as per 1 Corinthians 11:28. Secondly, it maintains the theological truth of the priesthood of all believers. As such it removes any notion of some mediatorial role for the priest or minister between God and the laity. This is a sacrament for the whole church and the whole sacrament ought to be given to each member of the congregation.

The Venerable Kara Hartley *is the Archdeacon for Women's Ministry in the Diocese of Sydney, Australia.*

QUESTIONS FOR REFLECTION

1. Why is it important for people to receive both the bread and the wine in the Supper?
2. Why is it important that there is only one mediator between God and us?
3. How should health and safety concerns affect the way we celebrate the Lord's Supper?

PRAYER

Heavenly Father, you have given to us the spiritual food of the most precious body and blood of our Saviour Jesus Christ to assure us of your favour and goodness towards us: purify our consciences from dead works that we may continue in the holy fellowship of your church, through Jesus Christ our Lord. *Amen.*

BIBLE READING

Hebrews 9:24-28

For Christ has entered, not into holy places made with hands, which are copies of the true things, but into heaven itself, now to appear in the presence of God on our behalf. Nor was it to offer himself repeatedly, as the high priest enters the holy places every year with blood not his own, for then he would have had to suffer repeatedly since the foundation of the world. But as it is, he has appeared once for all at the end of the ages to put away sin by the sacrifice of himself. And just as it is appointed for man to die once, and after that comes judgment, so Christ, having been offered once to bear the sins of many, will appear a second time, not to deal with sin but to save those who are eagerly waiting for him.

STARTER QUESTION

How is Christ's sacrifice different to the Old Testament sacrifices made by priests in the Temple?

ARTICLE XXXI

OF THE ONE OBLATION OF CHRIST FINISHED UPON THE CROSS

~

The Offering of Christ once made is that perfect redemption, propitiation, and satisfaction, for all the sins of the whole world, both original and actual; and there is none other satisfaction for sin, but that alone. Wherefore the sacrifices of Masses, in the which it was commonly said, that the Priest did offer Christ for the quick and the dead, to have remission of pain or guilt, were blasphemous fables, and dangerous deceits.

ARTICLE XXXI

Article 31 is the last of the Articles dealing with the sacraments (25-31). Yet the first sentence is so obviously related to the work of Christ and its soteriological significance that it almost feels like it belongs with the Articles which deal with the doctrine of salvation through Christ alone (11-18). This is an example of the interrelated nature of Christian doctrine and the way the sacramental teaching of the church has the potential to undermine wider theological foundations.

THE ROMAN MASS

The practices of the medieval church, and the conciliar endorsement they received at Trent in the years immediately preceding Cranmer's composition of this Article, are an apt example of this potential becoming a reality. The Roman church held—indeed, it continues to hold—that in the Mass, the substance of the bread and the wine changes to become the body and blood of Jesus Christ. As such, in the event of the Mass, the sacrifice Christ made is offered again to God and its benefits are received by those present. The Reformers rejected this teaching as both unbiblical and blasphemous. On the contrary, as Article 31 makes abundantly clear, the offering of Christ was made once and that unique event alone is the ground of a sinner's salvation.

The notion of continually offering sacrifices for sins is established by God for the Israelites in the Old Testament. However, the author of Hebrews makes clear that Jesus's sacrifice was unlike those made in the Levitical sacrificial system. 'He does not need to offer sacrifices day after day, first for his own sins, and then for the sins of the people. He sacrificed for their sins once for all when he offered himself' (Hebrews 7:27). Jesus is now in heaven, but 'he did not enter heaven to offer himself again and again... But he has appeared once and for all at the culmination of the ages to do away with sin by the sacrifice of himself' (Hebrews 9:26-27).

In other words, Jesus fulfils the system of perpetual offerings in his unique sacrifice where he was both priest and victim. To suggest that he needs to be offered over and over again undermines the achievement of the cross.

What did the Cross Achieve?

Article 31 describes Jesus' offering as achieving 'perfect redemption, propitiation, and satisfaction, for all the sins of the whole world, both original and actual.' This succinct expression of deep theological truths could hardly be stated with more acuity. It makes clear three achievements of the cross.

1. *Perfect Redemption* picks up the biblical idea being bought out of slavery. An important aspect of this concept is that there has been a transfer of ownership. The Hebrews in Exodus once belonged to Pharaoh but, after crossing the Red Sea, God made clear that they were now his treasured possession (Exodus 19:5). So also Paul states that Christians were once slaves to sin but they have been set free from sin to be slaves to God which leads to holiness and results in eternal life (Romans 6:22, cf. John 8:31-36).

2. *Propitiation* refers to the appeasing of God's wrath. In much that passes for theology these days, this concept has been repudiated. The truth that God is love is juxtaposed with the biblical testimony that God is angry at sin. Despite the offence it causes to modern sensibilities, both the Roman church and the Reformers were correct in their understanding that God is loving *and* angry

at sin. Indeed, his wrath results from his love. The unloving thing would have been to be apathetic to the disastrous effects of sin. But the testimony of Scripture is that God, motivated by love and mercy, propitiates his own wrath against sinners, by the blood of Christ Jesus (Romans 3:25; 1 John 2:2).

3. *Satisfaction* is making clear that the just punishment that was borne by Christ for sin has been entirely exhausted. There is nothing left to pay. There is no need for further offerings such as those represented in the Roman Mass. Christ's once-and-for-all offering of himself on the cross is all that is necessary (Hebrews 7-9).

Article 31 goes on to make clear that these achievements dealt with the problem of sin. Sin enslaved people who needed redemption. Sin caused God's wrath which needed propitiation. And sin deserved punishment which needed satisfaction.

Christ did this 'for all the sins of the whole world, both original and actual.' This phrase is pointing to the fact that because of who Christ is—God incarnate—one man's act of obedience could make many righteous (Romans 5:19). There is no sin a Christian can commit that is not atoned for in Christ's death. Furthermore, there is no Christian anywhere in the world whose sin is not atoned for in Christ's death. It is utterly sufficient for all.

Unlike the opinion prevalent in contemporary society, Article 31 is frank about the reality, the pervasiveness, and the consequences of sin. At the same time, the point of the Article is the unique and wonderful achievement of Christ in dealing with the problem of sin.

FREEDOM AND JOY IN CHRIST ALONE!

There are numerous applications from the doctrine articulated in Article 31. These include freedom from feelings of guilt that result from sin and rejoicing fervently at the achievement of Christ's atoning work.

However, the Article was written to combat the notion that something other than Christ's death (the Mass) could offer remission of guilt and it is at this point we should heed the Article's teaching. We can easily fall into the trap of thinking that when we sin we need to do something to make up for it: we need to read our Bible more, we need to be more involved at church, or we need to give more to charity. These are all good things, but none of them removes the guilt of our sin. Christ's death alone achieves this and as a result we are called to entrust ourselves to him alone.

The Revd Dr Ed Loane *is Lecturer in Theology and Church History at Moore Theological College, Sydney and author of William Temple and Church Unity: The Politics and Practice of Ecumenical Theology.*

QUESTIONS FOR REFLECTION

1. Why is the Mass said to be a blasphemous fable and dangerous deceit?
2. In what ways is the work of Christ on the cross 'perfect'?
3. How else might we be tempted to make satisfaction for our sin?

PRAYER

Father Almighty, whose Son Jesus Christ offered a full, perfect, and sufficient sacrifice and satisfaction for all our sins upon the cross: protect us from the devices and desires of our own deceitful hearts and keep us always in the joy of your salvation, through Jesus Christ our Saviour. *Amen.*

Bible Reading

1 Timothy 3:1-7

The saying is trustworthy: If anyone aspires to the office of overseer, he desires a noble task. Therefore an overseer must be above reproach, the husband of one wife, sober-minded, self-controlled, respectable, hospitable, able to teach, not a drunkard, not violent but gentle, not quarrelsome, not a lover of money. He must manage his own household well, with all dignity keeping his children submissive, for if someone does not know how to manage his own household, how will he care for God's church? He must not be a recent convert, or he may become puffed up with conceit and fall into the condemnation of the devil. Moreover, he must be well thought of by outsiders, so that he may not fall into disgrace, into a snare of the devil.

Starter Question

What sort of person should a minister of the church be?

ARTICLE XXXII

OF THE MARRIAGE OF PRIESTS

~

Bishops, Priests, and Deacons, are not
commanded by God's Law, either to vow
the estate of single life, or to abstain from
marriage: therefore it is lawful for them,
as for all other Christian men, to marry at
their own discretion, as they shall judge the
same to serve better to godliness.

ARTICLE XXXII

The effect of this Article is to put marriage and singleness on the same spiritual plane in the Church of England.

Singleness, which means a calling not to enter sexual relations, which we also call 'celibacy', had become the rule for clergy in the medieval Roman Catholic Church, and remains the rule there today. But as it appears in the New Testament that those in Christian leadership could be married (1 Timothy 3:1-13) and the Reformation wanted to put Scripture back as the supreme authority for the Church (see Articles 6 and 20), so marriage was to be made possible for the clergy—whose conduct was to be on the same level as 'for all other Christian men.'

In this respect the Article is saying there is no difference between clergy and laity; what matters is God's law and godliness for everyone in the Church, and as far as sex is concerned that means singleness or marriage.

CELIBACY

It's worth noting that the elevation of celibacy for the clergy developed quite early on in the Church's life. Jesus and Paul were of course celibate, even though in Jewish culture marriage was regarded as normal. As the Church grew into the Gentile world, there were many other kinds of sexual relationships going on (see 1 Corinthians 6:9-11) and in 1 Corinthians 7 Paul addresses the challenges of Christian ministry and the call to singleness or marriage.

There were good reasons why Christian ministers could be celibate which gradually took hold in the early centuries until it became a badge of special holiness to be single. The new monastic communities expressed this in the vows of poverty, chastity, and obedience.

In welcoming the biblical rebalancing of Article 32, it's worth us asking whether we haven't, in recovering marriage, lost something of that honouring of the single life. But the Bible does honour marriage, and the Article allows clergy to bear witness to that goodness as much as any other Christian.

DISCRETION TO DEFINE?

But some think that the phrase 'at their own discretion' means we can decide what marriage is as well as who we marry. Mike Ovey, in an article from *Themelios* in 2013 ('Colonial Atheism: A Very British Vice') refers to the UK government's legislation on same sex marriage as in effect saying 'marriage belongs to the UK Government. It *belongs* to it in the sense it has the right to define and shape it. It has the right to *name* what is and is not marriage.'

That is not how Article 32 sees marriage. For the Article, marriage and singleness are defined and shaped and 'named' by God through his law and commandments. The doctrine of marriage assumed by the Article is that set out in the Book of Common Prayer service, 'The solemnisation of holy matrimony', which includes a beautiful description of marriage as well as this distinction: 'For be ye well assured, that so many as are coupled together otherwise than God's word doth allow are not joined together by God; neither is their matrimony lawful.' Same-sex marriage may be lawful to the state, but that does not make it lawful to God.

MARRIAGE AND GODLINESS

God's law and commandment are the ground of the truth of marriage, and the goal is godliness. The question, unusual to modern ears, as to whether I should marry or stay single, as well as whether it is allowed by God's law, is: 'will marriage or singleness make me more godly?'

Perhaps you think this is all very well, but what about the real challenges of marriage and singleness? Those who formulated this Article were well aware of the challenges facing the married and the single. If you want to see how marriage in the sixteenth century fared in comparison with the twenty-first century, you may like to read the Homily on Matrimony in the *Second Book of Homilies* (1571) which includes the following salutary reminder of the pressures,

> ... we see how wonderfully the devil deludeth and scorneth this state, how few matrimonies there be without chidings, brawlings, tauntings, repentings, bitter cursings, and fightings. Which things whosoever doth commit, they do not consider that it is the instigation of the ghostly enemy, who taketh great delight therein: for else they would with all earnest endeavour strive against these mischiefs, not only with prayer, but also with all possible diligence.

The remainder of the Homily is devoted to what that prayer and diligence might look like.

PRAYING IN THE LIGHT OF THIS ARTICLE

Reading the Article today we might pray for Bishops, Priests, and Deacons we know, married and single. We might pray for all, whatever state they are in, whether married or single. We might ask whether we are doing enough to honour those who 'vow the estate of the single life.' Perhaps the Prayer Book could have included a service to solemnise that vow, or perhaps the Church should do so now?

Article 32 was very much a reaction to an abuse in the Church in the past. But we could pray for the abuses that threaten the life of the Church today in relation to marriage, praying for the authority and truth of scripture to shape our common life now as then, that in our experience of Christian marriage amongst the ordained and all Christian people, we may be grounded in God's law and commandments and come to serve better to godliness.

The Rt Revd Keith Sinclair *is the Bishop of Birkenhead and wrote two chapters in The Effective Anglican: Seizing the Opportunities of Ministry in the Church of England.*

QUESTIONS FOR REFLECTION

1. Does your church have a preference for single ministers or married ministers? Why?
2. How high a priority is it for people in your church to have relationships (of all kinds) which foster godliness?
3. Where is the authority of scripture to shape our common life under threat today in the areas of sex and marriage?

PRAYER

Heavenly Father, who has sanctified the marriage of
husband and wife as a sign of the covenant between
Christ and his church: grant to all those so married
that living faithfully together in peace, they may keep
the vows they have made; and give grace to us all that
we may so live together in this life, after the pattern
of Christ and his godly ministers, that in the world
to come we may enjoy the life eternal, through Jesus
Christ our Lord. *Amen.*

Bible Reading

Matthew 18:15-20

If your brother sins against you, go and tell him his fault, between you and him alone. If he listens to you, you have gained your brother. But if he does not listen, take one or two others along with you, that every charge may be established by the evidence of two or three witnesses. If he refuses to listen to them, tell it to the church. And if he refuses to listen even to the church, let him be to you as a Gentile and a tax collector. Truly, I say to you, whatever you bind on earth shall be bound in heaven, and whatever you loose on earth shall be loosed in heaven. Again I say to you, if two of you agree on earth about anything they ask, it will be done for them by my Father in heaven. For where two or three are gathered in my name, there am I among them.

Starter Question

How should we deal with unrepentant sinners in the church?

ARTICLE XXXIII

OF EXCOMMUNICATE PERSONS, HOW THEY ARE TO BE AVOIDED

~

That person which by open denunciation of the Church is rightly cut off from the unity of the Church, and excommunicated, ought to be taken of the whole multitude of the faithful, as an Heathen and Publican, until he be openly reconciled by penance, and received into the Church by a Judge that hath authority thereunto.

ARTICLE XXXIII

The discipline of the medieval Church had grown out of the godly, if severe, practices of the early Church in restoring sinners and apostates to its fellowship. In the course of time, however, it had not only become extremely burdensome but also casuistical and corrupt. The Reformers were, understandably, wary of such legalism and excess of discipline, especially if one could buy oneself out of any discipline that was imposed! They raised their voice against such corruption and abuse of discipline, but not discipline itself.

The Necessity of Discipline

The Anglican Reformers were critical of Rome's excessive discipline at the time but the formularies all recognise the necessity of sufficient and godly discipline in the Church. The *Book of Common Prayer*, for instance, in the rubric at the beginning of the service of Holy Communion, sets out the possibility of the 'lesser excommunication' or suspension from receiving Holy Communion for those who are 'open and notorious evil livers' and/or have somehow wronged their neighbours, without making restitution. The Ordinal also charges those being ordained priest or consecrated bishop 'to banish and drive away all erroneous and strange doctrines contrary to God's Word.'

Aside from Article 33, to which we shall presently come, Article 26 famously teaches that 'the unworthiness of the ministers hinders not the effect of the Sacrament.' It also declares that such unworthy ministers should be disciplined through due process. Martin Davie in his commentary on the Articles helpfully lists a number of canons in the Canons of 1604 which prescribe discipline. He points out that these canons distinguish between the 'lesser excommunication' i.e. suspension from receiving Holy Communion and the 'greater excommunication' which would carry heavier penalties. Present day Canons of the Church of England reflect such discipline without, perhaps, distinguishing so clearly between the different kinds of excommunication.

This brings us to the somewhat uncompromising wording of Article 33. In the background here is the authority given in the New Testament to the Church and her leaders to 'bind and to loose', to 'forgive and to retain' sins (Matthew 16:13-20, John 20:19-23). The specific passage alluded to in the Article seems to be Matthew 18:15-20 where, if an errant brother does not listen even to the Church, he is to be regarded as a Heathen and a Publican.

This is, in its Jewish context, would have meant one with whom there is no spiritual or social intercourse. Such teaching is, of course, reflected in what St Paul says about the treatment of someone in a state of grave sin (1 Corinthians 5:1-13). The Article, then, seems to be going beyond the communion rubric and to be referring to a 'greater excommunication.'

As the Reformation historian, James Atkinson, has shown in his *Martin Luther and the Birth of Protestantism*, one of the issues which Luther confronted was how the commuting of a disciplinary penalty passed from the whole congregation to the pastors and bishops and from thence to a rapidly centralising papacy. Neither Luther nor the Article is denying that there are those in the Church who have legitimate authority to impose and to relax discipline.

RESTORING THE PENITENT

Unlike some in the Radical Reformation, the mainstream Reformers did not deny what the Article asserts, that the penalty of even the greater excommunication might be relaxed by 'a judge that hath authority thereunto.'

This is, in fact, the most important element in Church discipline of any kind: the aim to bring the offender to repentance and, eventually, to restoration. In this sense, all discipline must be motivated by love and the desire to see the offender return home. For this reason also, unless there are serious fears for the safety of others, no one under discipline should be prevented from attending divine worship and from listening to the word of God read and preached. Whether 1 Corinthians 5:1-5 and 2 Corinthians 2:5-11 are about the same or different persons, the aim in both accounts is the salvation and the restoration of the offender to fellowship with Christ and with his body, the Church.

It is in this light that the controversy in the early Church about those who had apostatised in a period of persecution, is to be read. The consensus, as it emerged, was that they could be received back after due discipline, to be determined on a case by case basis, had been exercised. Any church worthy of that name should have procedures both for determining what discipline is required for this or that offence *and* for the restoration of the penitent.

AVOIDING FALSE TEACHERS

We should not forget a special category of those who are to be avoided: those who hold or teach false beliefs or who deny apostolic authority (e.g. Romans 16:17-18, 2 Thessalonians 3:14, Titus 3:10, 2 John 10,11). That is to say, there can be doctrinal as well as moral reasons for excommunication. It should be a matter of huge disappointment to faithful Anglicans that the General Synod of the Church of England, whilst agreeing a disciplinary procedure for clergy on moral issues, refused to do so for matters of doctrine, thus leaving the Church with only antiquated and extremely expensive processes for dealing with discipline on doctrine.

This is especially disappointing because the clergy are involved: that is, the very people who have the responsibility of preaching the Word 'in season and out of season' (2 Timothy 4:2). Both 1 Timothy and Titus show how bishops and presbyters are to hold and teach the Faith in its wholeness. From St Cyprian we know that the early Church was hostile even to the ministry of those bishops and clergy who had apostatised under persecution. How is doctrinal fitness to exercise episcopal or presbyteral office in the Church of England to be determined in the absence of any process?

CHURCH DISCIPLINE TODAY

The new liturgies of the Church of England do not mention excommunication and the present Canons only mention suspension from Holy Communion. Yet the Book of Common Prayer remains the doctrinal and liturgical standard for the Church of England— and its references to discipline, suspension from Communion, and excommunication as such remain in force and should be taken seriously by both clergy and laity.

Because of the establishment of the Church of England, excommunication also originally carried with it a number of civil exclusions and penalties. Until the early nineteenth century, excommunication was a common penalty for contempt of both ecclesiastical and civil courts. This is, rightly, no longer the case with civil litigation but the Church continues to have responsibility for its own discipline.

As E. J. Bicknell points out in his well known work *A Theological Introduction to the Thirty-nine Articles of the Church of England*, 'we need a fresh recognition of the holiness which is required of Church members.' This is not a counsel of perfection nor a demand for a perfect Church, but it takes seriously the need for faithful discipleship and acknowledges that membership of the Church carries definite obligations. This is also true *a fortiori* of those who have responsibilities for teaching, preaching, and leading.

The present crisis in the Anglican Communion has arisen from a refusal to exercise godly discipline whether for individuals, office holders, dioceses, or even provinces. We must have prayerful, biblical, and robust structures of effective discipline in place at every level of church life. Otherwise, churches as well as the Anglican Communion as a whole will lurch from one emergency to another. This is deeply damaging for the faithful, in their growth in faith, hope, and love, and for the Church as an institution that is effective, consistent, and credible.

In its own austere way, Article 33 shows us a painful but necessary part of church life. We need not use its language but its intention is biblical and asks sharp questions about the state of discipline in the Church today. Have we any answers to give and provision to make?

The Rt Revd Dr Michael Nazir-Ali *is the Director of OXTRAD, a former Bishop of Rochester, and author of Faith, Freedom and the Future: Challenges for the 21st Century.*

QUESTIONS FOR REFLECTION

1. What procedures does your church have for determining when and what discipline is required for various offences, and for restoring those who are penitent?
2. How do we see discipline exercised against false teachers in the church today?
3. What are some of the difficulties of exercising effective church discipline?

PRAYER

Loving Father, for our good you discipline those you receive as children that we might share in your holiness: grant us repentance and a knowledge of the truth that by your Spirit we may bring forth the peaceable fruit of righteousness, and our churches may be filled with the truth that leads to godliness, though Christ our Lord. *Amen.*

Bible Reading

1 Corinthians 14:26-33

What then, brothers? When you come together, each one has a hymn, a lesson, a revelation, a tongue, or an interpretation. Let all things be done for building up. If any speak in a tongue, let there be only two or at most three, and each in turn, and let someone interpret. But if there is no one to interpret, let each of them keep silent in church and speak to himself and to God. Let two or three prophets speak, and let the others weigh what is said. If a revelation is made to another sitting there, let the first be silent. For you can all prophesy one by one, so that all may learn and all be encouraged, and the spirits of prophets are subject to prophets. For God is not a God of confusion but of peace.

Starter Question

What overarching principles does the Apostle give the Corinthians for thinking about what happens at their gatherings?

ARTICLE XXXIV

OF THE TRADITIONS
OF THE CHURCH

~

It is not necessary that Traditions and Ceremonies
be in all places one, and utterly like; for at all
times they have been divers, and may be changed
according to the diversities of countries, times, and
men's manners, so that nothing be ordained against
God's Word.
Whosoever through his private judgement, willingly
and purposely, doth openly break the traditions and
ceremonies of the Church, which be not repugnant
to the Word of God, and be ordained and approved
by common authority, ought to be rebuked openly,
(that others may fear to do the like,) as he that
offendeth against the common order of the Church,
and hurteth the authority of the Magistrate, and
woundeth the consciences of the weak brethren.
Every particular or national Church hath authority
to ordain, change, and abolish, ceremonies or rites
of the Church ordained only by man's authority, so
that all things be done to edifying.

ARTICLE XXXIV

Article 34 tackles the question of uniformity of traditions in the Church, drawing on what has already been established concerning the authority of Scripture (Article 6) and of the church (Article 20). The parallel of 'Traditions and Ceremonies' in the first sentence with 'ceremonies or rites' in the last, makes clear that the 'Traditions of the Church' this Article is concerned with are those of practices, not of doctrines: those 'ordained only by man's authority' and not by the authority of Scripture.

The Articles have been clear and firm on essential doctrine. But equally clear and firm on the boundary to what is essential. Scripture is sufficient, but not exhaustive. Here, beyond that boundary, in the land of non-essentials—things on which we may differ— Article 34 gives us principles for navigation.

NON-NEGOTIABLE PRINCIPLES

Before we discuss the principles and their value for today, however, it is well worth us noting the two non-negotiables this Article gives us, even as we set foot in the land of non-essentials. The first is the concern that 'nothing be ordained against God's Word'—taking us right back to Article 6. For the English Reformers, Scripture is paramount. Our doctrine is established by Scripture and our practice is to be held up and examined in its light. Practice that is found to be contrary to Scripture is therefore wrong, but we cannot immediately rule-out a practice which is not contrary to Scripture.

The second non-negotiable comes at the end of the Article, 'that all things be done to edifying.' The language here is most likely from 1 Corinthians 14:26 (see also Romans 14:19) where, addressing what happens when God's people meet together, Paul insists that everything that is done must be done for the purpose of 'building up.' So, when considering an aspect of our life together and whether to ordain, change, or abolish a particular practice, the Church must decide whether a course of action will build up believers in their relationship with God.

Commenting on this Article, W. H. Griffith Thomas concludes that 'we are neither to adhere obstinately to anything ancient simply because it is ancient, nor rashly to introduce anything novel because it is new. In everything connected with ceremonies or rites the ruling principle of spiritual edification is to be kept in mind.'

So on the one hand our practices must not go against God's word, and on the other hand they must be for the building up of God's people. Of course this leaves us with lots of freedom: how much water we use for baptism, how many passages of Scripture we read in a service, how frequently we gather for the Lord's Supper, what posture we should assume when praying in a service, what a minister ought to wear, and so on. But Article 34 helps us further, providing us with two principles for navigation.

NAVIGATING DISAGREEMENT ON NON-ESSENTIALS

First: 'It is not necessary that Traditions and Ceremonies be in all places one, or utterly like.' The Church does not have to take the same approach to a given area of practice at all times and in all places. It is perfectly acceptable to reach different conclusions in different places or at different times. Context matters and so long as the Church is not acting contrary to Scripture and is acting for the building up of God's people, different contexts may lead to different conclusions when it comes to practice.

In its original context, this principle was to justify change in practice against the objections of Rome. With the growth of the Church amidst increasing fragmentation across Europe, the Reformers insisted on the right of each national church to make its own decisions on matters of practice.

Second, individuals must not 'openly break the traditions and ceremonies of the Church, which be not repugnant to the Word of God, and be ordained and approved by common authority,' that is, practices which have been properly established. The *Book of Common Prayer* statement 'Of Ceremonies' takes us again to 1 Corinthians 14 and Paul's exhortation that 'all things be done among you in a seemly and due order' (1 Corinthians 14:40). Our Article takes Paul's concern seriously, hence the open rebuke due to anyone who opposes a properly established practice.

Applying Article 34 Today

What of this Article's value today? First, whilst certain revisionists seek to assure us that some 'accommodation' within our practice does not change our doctrine, it is vital for us to insist that in our practice as well as our doctrine, 'nothing be ordained against God's Word.'

Second, whilst the word of God never changes, we are reminded that tradition is always contextual and we must not lose sight of the priority of the edification of God's people in our own time and place.

Third, in our era of world-cities and multiculturalism we may well have questions over the legitimacy of practice being determined by the national church. But in our era of individualism and consumerism, this Article surely has great value in calling us back to 'due order.' Whilst the Reformers oppose the uniformity of Rome in this Article and give us various reasons for variety in practice, there is no suggestion that we should embrace difference merely to be different. Might it not do us—and the watching world—good if, where we can, we stand in line with those who have gone before us, maintaining the 'common order of the Church'?

The Revd James Taylor *is the Associate Rector of the Parish of St Helier, Jersey, the Vice Chairman of Church Society Council, and wrote the opening chapter in* Positively Anglican: Building on the Foundations and Transforming the Church.

QUESTIONS FOR REFLECTION

1. What diversity of traditions have you seen in different church services?
2. How should we evaluate our own traditions and rituals?
3. When should we abandon traditional or customary practices in the church?

PRAYER

Lord Jesus Christ, in whom the church is being built together as a dwelling place for God by the Spirit: help us maintain the unity of the Spirit in the bond of peace and speak the truth in love that we may declare the manifold wisdom of the God and Father of us all, who is over all and through all and in all. *Amen.*

BIBLE READING

1 Timothy 4:11-15

Command and teach these things. Let no one despise you for your youth, but set the believers an example in speech, in conduct, in love, in faith, in purity. Until I come, devote yourself to the public reading of Scripture, to exhortation, to teaching. Do not neglect the gift you have, which was given you by prophecy when the council of elders laid their hands on you. Practice these things, immerse yourself in them, so that all may see your progress. Keep a close watch on yourself and on the teaching. Persist in this, for by so doing you will save both yourself and your hearers.

STARTER QUESTION

What several things does the Apostle say here about ministers speaking in church?

Article XXXV

OF THE HOMILIES

~

The second Book of Homilies, the several titles whereof we have joined under this Article, doth contain a godly and wholesome Doctrine, and necessary for these times, as doth the former Book of Homilies, which were set forth in the time of Edward the Sixth; and therefore we judge them to be read in Churches by the Ministers, diligently and distinctly, that they may be understood of the people.

Of the Names of the Homilies

1. Of the right Use of the Church.

2. Against peril of Idolatry.

3. Of repairing and keeping clean of Churches.

4. Of good Works: first of Fasting.

5. Against Gluttony and Drunkenness.

6. Against Excess of Apparel.

7. Of Prayer.

8. Of the Place and Time of Prayer.

9. That Common Prayers and Sacraments ought to be ministered in a known tongue.

10. Of the reverend estimation of God's Word.

11. Of Alms-doing.

12. Of the Nativity of Christ.

13. Of the Passion of Christ.

14. Of the Resurrection of Christ.

15. Of the worthy receiving of the Sacrament of the Body and Blood of Christ.

16. Of the Gifts of the Holy Ghost.

17. For the Rogation-days.

18. Of the State of Matrimony.

19. Of Repentance.

20. Against Idleness.

21. Against Rebellion.

ARTICLE XXXV

Article 35 reminds us that there are two books of Homilies, or Sermons, first issued in 1547 and 1563 respectively, that form part of the basic documents of the Church of England. They are of considerable importance for understanding both its history and its doctrine, but few people now read them, and to all practical purposes they have gone out of use in the church.

In some ways this is a pity, because the Church of England was the only branch of Reformed Christendom that incorporated sermons into its statements of faith, reminding us that what we believe must also be applied in our lives. The Homilies are thematic in nature, which makes them especially important for establishing the Church's doctrine and shaping its practice.

The Content of the Homilies

Some of the Homilies expound the great doctrinal themes of the Reformation for the benefit of those who did not understand why the church had changed. They expound the nature and use of Holy Scripture, the fall of mankind, salvation by Christ, the relationship between faith and good works, and the central importance of love in the Christian life.

Others are disciplinary, designed to raise the moral and spiritual standards of church members who were prone to swearing, brawling and other forms of anti-social behaviour. There is an entire cycle in the second book that covers the main festivals of the Christian year from Christmas to Pentecost, teaching us what they mean and why we should continue to celebrate them.

In addition to these, there are miscellaneous Homilies that deal with subjects like marriage and adultery, the need for repentance, and the danger of idleness. A few are dedicated to the devotional life of prayer, fasting, and public worship, including the need to be reverent in church and to avoid venerating relics and statues, a medieval practice that was regarded as a form of idolatry. Finally, two of the Homilies are openly political, preaching in favour of civil obedience and against rebellion.

The Purpose of the Homilies

Sixteenth-century England was a rough place in many ways, and the Homilies were designed to inculcate Christian behaviour in everyday life. Some of them, like the one for Rogation Sunday, seem rather quaint today, but the doctrinal sermons are still as fresh as they were when they were first written.

The Homilies were intended to provide churchgoers with teaching about what the Church of England stood for and why it had embraced the Reformation. Thanks to them, the sermon as a means of establishing what we believe and communicating it to church members was deeply ingrained in the Anglican psyche, and it has always been central to our devotional life. Modern congregations are unlikely to read or listen to the Homilies in their original form, although the language is not nearly as old-fashioned as we might think. The problem is that some of them are very long and the formal style of writing is hard for us to follow in the age of the sound bite.

Using the Homilies Today

But this does not mean that the Homilies are of no use to us now. Properly adapted and mined for hidden treasures, modern preachers can still use them as a resource for their own sermons. They remind us that the teaching role of the church covers every aspect of the Christian life and cannot be reduced to a few favourite topics.

The Homilies keep us on our toes as Christians and continue to challenge what we believe and how we behave, reminding us that the one leads to the other and that we need both if we are going to live in a way that will bring glory to God.

The Revd Professor Gerald Bray *is Director of Research at the Latimer Trust, the Editor of Churchman, and author of A Fruitful Exhortation: A Guide to the Homilies.*

Questions for Reflection

1. How can preachers today ensure they cover the same wide range of doctrines and subjects as the Homilies?
2. How might it be useful today to read the sermons of Reformation-era Anglicans?
3. How important is preaching in the life of your church?

Prayer

Almighty God, whose unerring word is living and active, trustworthy and true to train us in righteousness: empower and enable our preachers so to wield the sword of the Spirit which is the word of God that we may be wise for salvation in Christ and equipped for every good work, to the glory of your name. *Amen.*

BIBLE READING:

2 Timothy 1:6-12

For this reason I remind you to fan into flame the gift of God, which is in you through the laying on of my hands, for God gave us a spirit not of fear but of power and love and self-control. Therefore do not be ashamed of the testimony about our Lord, nor of me his prisoner, but share in suffering for the gospel by the power of God, who saved us and called us to a holy calling, not because of our works but because of his own purpose and grace, which he gave us in Christ Jesus before the ages began, and which now has been manifested through the appearing of our Saviour Christ Jesus, who abolished death and brought life and immortality to light through the gospel, for which I was appointed a preacher and apostle and teacher, which is why I suffer as I do.

STARTER QUESTION

Why did Timothy need the spirit of power and love and self-control as a minister of the gospel?

ARTICLE XXXVI

OF THE CONSECRATION OF BISHOPS AND MINISTERS

~

The Book of Consecration of Archbishops and Bishops, and Ordering of Priests and Deacons, lately set forth in the time of Edward the Sixth, and confirmed at the same time by authority of Parliament, doth contain all things necessary to such Consecration and Ordering: neither hath it any thing, that of itself is superstitious and ungodly. And therefore whosoever are consecrated and ordered according to the Rites of that Book, since the second year of the forenamed King Edward unto this time, or hereafter shall be consecrated or ordered according to the same Rites; we decree all such to be rightly, orderly, and lawfully consecrated and ordered.

ARTICLE XXXVI

As Rod Thomas has already made clear, Article 23 asserts the need for those who assume the office of public preaching or ministering the Sacraments in the Congregation to be 'lawfully called and sent to execute the same.' This means being 'chosen and called to this work by men who have publick authority given unto them in the Congregation, to call and send Ministers into the Lord's vineyard.' There must be a process of discerning those with the qualifications for public ministry (cf. 1 Timothy 3:1-13), and a form of authorisation by those who constitute 'the body of elders' (1 Timothy 4:14; 5:22). The laying-on of hands with prayer is central to this authorisation for leadership in various New Testament contexts (see also Acts 6:6; 14:23). Article 36 simply affirms the validity and sufficiency of the ordination services in the Book of Common Prayer for the formal calling and sending of those qualified for office in the Church of England.

HISTORY

There was no Ordinal in the first English Prayer Book (1549), but *The Form and Manner of Making and Consecrating of Archbishops, Bishops, Priests, and Deacons* was published in 1550. This was an original composition, reflecting more biblical views about the nature and purpose of these ministries. However, it retained certain customs that had arisen during the Middle Ages, such as giving the Priest the Bible in one hand and the chalice or cup with the bread in the other, accompanied by the words 'Take authority to preach the word of God, and to minister the holy Sacraments in this congregation, where thou shalt be so appointed.' Different vestments were prescribed for the different orders of ministry, and in the form of consecrating an Archbishop or Bishop a Bible was laid upon the candidate's neck and a pastoral staff was put into his hands.

A revised ordinal was published as part of the new Prayer Book in 1552 in which these customs were removed. The services remained virtually unchanged until 1662, when certain verbal modifications were made, the age of Deacons was raised from twenty-one to twenty-three, Deacons were restricted to baptising 'in the absence of the Priest', new lessons and collects were added, directions about the vesture of Bishops were given, and the words of ordination were expanded.

Based on the words of Jesus to his disciples in John 20:22-23, the Bishop was now to say to each of the candidates for the Order of Priesthood, 'Receive the Holy Ghost for the Office and Work of a Priest in the Church of God, *now committed unto thee by the Imposition of our hands.* Whose sins thou dost forgive, they are forgiven; and whose sins thou dost retain, they are retained. and be thou a faithful Dispenser of the Word of God, and of his holy Sacraments; In the Name of the Father, and of the Son, and of the Holy Ghost. Amen.'

Recalling Paul's words in 2 Timothy 1:6-7, Bishops were to be consecrated with the words, 'Receive the Holy Ghost for the Office and Work of a Bishop in the Church of God, *now committed unto thee by the Imposition of our hands; In the Name of the Father, and of the Son, and of the Holy Ghost. Amen. And remember that thou stir up the grace of God which is given thee by this Imposition of our hands*; for God hath not given us the spirit of fear, but of power, and love, and soberness.'

THEOLOGY AND INTENTION

Article 36, which dates from 1563, first seeks to deal with challenges about the validity of Anglican orders from Roman Catholics. It affirms that both Ordinals authorised in the time of Edward VI contain 'all things necessary' for the proper consecration of Archbishops and Bishops and the ordering of Priests and Deacons. Moreover, it asserts that those ordained according to those rites 'be rightly, orderly, and lawfully consecrated and ordered.'

Catholics have argued that our Ordinal is deficient because it has no provision for the anointing of the hands of priests and no delivery of the sacramental 'instruments' (the bread and the cup). They rightly discern that there is no intention in our liturgy to ordain candidates to a sacerdotal priesthood, involving the offering of a 'Eucharistic sacrifice.'

Article 36 also addresses challenges about the services containing 'any thing that of itself is superstitious and ungodly.' Puritan objections focused on the form of words used at the moment of ordination. Jesus's words 'Receive the Holy Ghost' were associated with his breathing on them as a sign that he would give them his Spirit. In the ordination services, these words function as 'wish-prayers' such as Paul used in his letters (e.g. Romans 15:5-6, 13). Although they are directed to the candidates, God is being asked to fill each one with his Spirit for the effective exercise of the ministry that is committed to them. Jesus' promise about forgiving or not forgiving sins relates to the ministry of the gospel (John 20:23; cf. Luke 24:47).

The exhortations and the questions put to the candidates in our services make it abundantly clear that the fundamental task of the minister is to labour at teaching, preaching, and applying the gospel. Declaring the forgiveness of sins to those who truly repent is a formal expression of this ministry when the church gathers, but it is not the main reason for quoting the words of Jesus to the candidates at their ordination.

CONTINUING RELEVANCE

Recent revisions of the Ordinal in the Anglican Communion have tended to re-introduce ceremonies and variations of vesture in line with the medieval traditions. Such changes are associated with modifications to the Communion services, giving expression to a theology of Eucharistic sacrifice and sacerdotal priesthood. But Article 36 reminds us that even the simplified Ordinal of 1552 contains 'all things necessary' for the proper consecration of Archbishops and Bishops and the ordering of Priests and Deacons.

Moreover, Article 36 continues to challenge those who think the ordination services contain superstitious and ungodly material to understand particular words and actions within the context of the liturgy as a whole.

The Revd Dr David Peterson *is the former Principal of Oak Hill Theological College, London and author of* Encountering God Together: Biblical Patterns for Ministry and Worship.

QUESTIONS FOR REFLECTION

1. Why is there a need for a public service and recognition of ordination?
2. Why is it especially important to ensure ordination services contain nothing 'that of itself is superstitious and ungodly'?
3. Does is matter that Roman Catholics think Anglican ordination is deficient?

PRAYER

Heavenly Father, you call all Bishops, Presbyters, and
Deacons to be messengers, watchmen, and stewards
of the Lord: grant them grace to shepherd willingly
and serve eagerly as examples to the flock and faithful
soldiers of Christ Jesus, that when the Chief Shepherd
appears they will receive the unfading crown of glory,
through the merits of Christ our Lord. *Amen.*

BIBLE READING

Romans 13:1-7

Let every person be subject to the governing authorities. For there is no authority except from God, and those that exist have been instituted by God. Therefore whoever resists the authorities resists what God has appointed, and those who resist will incur judgment. For rulers are not a terror to good conduct, but to bad. Would you have no fear of the one who is in authority? Then do what is good, and you will receive his approval, for he is God's servant for your good. But if you do wrong, be afraid, for he does not bear the sword in vain. For he is the servant of God, an avenger who carries out God's wrath on the wrongdoer. Therefore one must be in subjection, not only to avoid God's wrath but also for the sake of conscience. For because of this you also pay taxes, for the authorities are ministers of God, attending to this very thing. Pay to all what is owed to them: taxes to whom taxes are owed, revenue to whom revenue is owed, respect to whom respect is owed, honour to whom honour is owed.

STARTER QUESTION

Why should Christians obey the secular authorities of this world?

ARTICLE XXXVII

OF THE CIVIL MAGISTRATES

⁓

The King's Majesty hath the chief power in this Realm
of England, and other his Dominions, unto whom
the chief Government of all Estates of this Realm,
whether they be Ecclesiastical or Civil, in all causes
doth appertain, and is not, nor ought to be, subject
to any foreign Jurisdiction. Where we attribute to
the King's Majesty the chief government, by which
Titles we understand the minds of some slanderous
folks to be offended; we give not to our Princes the
ministering either of God's Word, or of the Sacraments,
the which thing the Injunctions also lately set forth
by Elizabeth our Queen do most plainly testify; but
that only prerogative, which we see to have been given
always to all godly Princes in holy Scriptures by God
himself; that is, that they should rule all estates and
degrees committed to their charge by God, whether
they be Ecclesiastical or Temporal, and restrain with the
civil sword the stubborn and evil-doers. The Bishop of
Rome hath no jurisdiction in this Realm of England.
The Laws of the Realm may punish Christian men with
death, for heinous and grievous offences. It is lawful
for Christian men, at the commandment of the
Magistrate, to wear weapons, and serve in the wars.

ARTICLE XXXVII

To our modern ears, Article 37 sounds a little strange, uncomfortable even. It first appeared in Archbishop Parker's reworking of the Articles in 1563, replacing a shorter and simpler statement on royal supremacy. Nevertheless Article 37's bold assertion that the 'King's Majesty hath the chief power in this Realm of England… whether they be Ecclesiastical or Civil…' is striking. The notion that the monarch has power over the church may well leave us wondering as to the applicability of Article 37 in our own times.

But before we dismiss Article 37, there are valuable insights here that rightly challenge some of our modern thinking. For sure, the Article must be approached with some caution, but that does not mean that the Article does not speak to us today.

THE BIBLICAL AND HISTORICAL CONTEXT

The context out of which the Article appears is key to reading rightly the intention behind what is being said. In a turbulent period of history, the Reformation in England began with a rejection of the Roman Church's assertion of supremacy over the temporal authority, namely the King. In short, Henry VIII's desire for divorce prompted a constitutional crisis when the Pope refused permission, prompting loud and outraged questions over his right to assert authority over the King. That history is reflected in the Article.

Article 37 draws on Matthew 22:15-22 (paying taxes to Caesar), Romans 13:1-7, and 1 Peter 2:13-17. Paul emphatically demands, 'Let every person be subject to the governing authorities. For there is no authority except from God, and those that exist have been instituted by God.' This is matched by Peter's insistence that his readers, 'Be subject for the Lord's sake to every human institution.' But exactly what does that mean?

By What Authority?

In the West today, we approach Article 37 in ways that divide the state and the church into two distinct categories. Contemporary society tells us that 'religion' is a private, individual matter and therefore seeks to push the church out of the public square. The reasons for this are varied, but assumptions of this kind force onto Article 37 a view of life that its framers could not (rightly) conceive.

We talk in terms that make strong distinctions between temporal and spiritual, but the Church Militant is 'here in earth' (as the Prayer Book puts it) and is thus manifested in a temporal realm. We cannot, as Oliver O'Donovan says in his book on the Articles, escape the State.

Rather than imposing our modern frame of reference on the text, O'Donovan helpfully speaks of two types of authority. The opening of Article 37 draws attention to the first kind: 'The King's Majesty hath the chief power in this Realm of England.' This is an Authority to Command. It is the government that bears responsibility for the ordering and shaping of society. The church, therefore, relies in general terms on government, as it is government that provides the context in which the visible church exists.

But that Authority to Command, absolute as it is, is restrained by a second authority, an Authority of Truth. It is to the Authority of Truth that the second part of Article 37 alludes: 'we give not to our Princes the ministering either of God's Word, or of the Sacraments.' This is an authority also considered elsewhere (Article 20), and it restrains the role of the government. The Church of England is a national church, not a state church. Indeed we may go further: the King's Majesty, the government, only has pre-eminence to command because of the prior Authority of Truth as set forth in scripture.

The position of Article 37 is helpfully summarized by O'Donovan: 'Society, then, is one society, and the monarch's writ runs everywhere within it, though always (and again, in every aspect of social life) subject to the critical authority of the word of God, which the monarch himself does not have the authority to expound or preach.'

The point is illustrated with the Article itself. We read that 'It is lawful for Christian men, at the commandment of the Magistrate, to wear weapons, and serve in the wars.' The law that gives the magistrate the right to command men to bear weapons must surely be the law of God itself. As a military chaplain, my desire to say more here is very great indeed! Suffice to say, it means that those operating in the military do not exercise authority in their own right and that the *lawful* fulfilment of military duties (including the taking of a life of others) is an action on behalf of the State.

And although less clearly asserted, the same logic must underpin the Article's belief that the government has the right to carry out the death penalty (though whether that is regularly today the most expedient course is another discussion).

THE CHURCH'S RIGHT TO SPEAK

In our own time, the Article is useful in that it pushes back against societal and cultural pressures that refuse the right of the church to be heard in the public square. Indeed, more than that: it refuses to accept that the church can only speak when legitimacy is granted by the state. Theologically it is the other way round. The right of the State to exercise the Authority to Command is a right given by the Authority of Truth. A thought, perhaps, to remember the next time the secularists invite us to leave our faith at the door.

The Revd Geoffrey Firth *is a RAF Chaplain at RAF Marham in Norfolk, and a member of the Church Society Council.*

QUESTIONS FOR REFLECTION

1. Does the church have a right to be heard in 'the public square'?
2. How might the authority of the state clash with 'the critical authority of the word of God'?
3. Is it possible to be a godly Christian serving in the military?

PRAYER

Almighty and everlasting God, ruler of all things in
heaven and on earth: we pray for monarchs, presidents,
and all who are in high positions, that your Holy
Spirit may in everything direct and rule their hearts so
that we may lead a peaceful and quiet life, godly and
dignified in every way, to the glory of your holy name.
Amen.

BIBLE READING

2 Corinthians 9:6-9

The point is this: whoever sows sparingly will also reap sparingly, and whoever sows bountifully will also reap bountifully. Each one must give as he has decided in his heart, not reluctantly or under compulsion, for God loves a cheerful giver. And God is able to make all grace abound to you, so that having all sufficiency in all things at all times, you may abound in every good work. As it is written,

> 'He has distributed freely, he has given to the poor;
> his righteousness endures forever.'

STARTER QUESTION

Why should Christians give generously to others?

ARTICLE XXXVIII

OF CHRISTIAN MEN'S GOODS, WHICH ARE NOT COMMON

~

The Riches and Goods of Christians
are not common, as touching the right,
title, and possession of the same, as
certain Anabaptists do falsely boast.
Notwithstanding, every man ought, of such
things as he possesseth, liberally to give alms
to the poor, according to his ability.

ARTICLE XXXVIII

Go back a generation or two and the Church of England was often labelled 'the Conservative Party at prayer.' More recently perceptions have changed and the left-wing bias of the established church (and most especially that of its bishops) has been the focus of much criticism—especially in the right-wing press. Reflecting on this transformation, no less an authoritative figure than Sir Humphrey Appleby posed this question in the 1980s BBC TV series *Yes Prime Minister*: 'Isn't it interesting how nowadays politicians talk about morals and bishops talk about politics?'

ANABAPTISTS AND PRIVATE PROPERTY
In Article 38 we have the Church of England of the first Elizabeth's reign talking both politics *and* morals. But it's the politics that—even then—comes first. The Reformation party in England are wanting to clearly distance themselves from the extremists of the continental Reformation—the Anabaptists. The Anabaptists had not only sought radical changes in the Christian religion (like believers' only baptism) but changes in the wider political and social orders too—including an end to the concept of private property (with Acts 4 as their biblical justification).

The Anabaptist seizure of the German city of Münster in 1534 had trialled this proto-communist approach to possessions and been bloodily repressed after a year-long siege. From then on religious reformers needed to reassure their political masters that they were most definitely in favour of property rights and would not seek any radical redistribution of wealth (most especially of anything belonging to these rulers).

The Church of England's leadership needed to clarify that they were just after religious reformation and no such wide-ranging political, economic, and social revolution; a more successful (but still not permanent) attempt at ending private property would have to wait a few centuries for the arrival of one Karl Marx. Then the advent of Communism would breathe new life into the first clause of Article 38 and seemingly justify accusations of the Anglican approach to politics being more to the right than the left.

THE BIBLICAL BALANCE

But actually Article 38 is both biblically and politically balanced. The generous giving and sharing of the early Christians was not driven by any ban on private ownership—in Acts 5 Peter makes it very clear to the deceitful Ananias and Sapphira that their property was their own to keep or give away as they chose to (Acts 5:4). It's not an individual's possession of money but their love of it that troubles the apostle Paul (1 Timothy 6:10). The first part of Article 38 would seem to be not just a politically expedient one but a justifiably biblical one too.

Any historic charges of Anglican right-wing bias are surely undermined by the second part of Article 38. Here generosity to the poor is simply expected with no insistence on the poor being 'deserving'—as has often been demanded by those on the political right. Instead the focus is on every individual giving in proportion to their own resources—the richer are given the clear moral duty of caring for all of those less fortunate than themselves.

Now the biblical warrant for this comes, of course, in the much-repeated commandment to love one's neighbour as oneself, and passages on the use of financial resources like 1 Timothy 6:17-

19. But in political terms the feel is of a much more left-wing sounding redistribution of wealth. The first clause of the Article might be understood as right-leaning, but the second could be seen to take things in the opposite direction.

Whatever the politics, the moral case is clearly made: I am biblically justified in owning things, but the Bible also demands that I share those things with those in need. The church of Jerusalem asked the apostle Paul to prioritise remembering the poor—something he was eager do (Galatians 6:10). The Church of England's foundational Articles of Religion ask all Anglicans to do the same—are we showing the same eagerness today?

Ed Shaw *is the Pastor of Emmanuel City Centre, an Anglican church-plant in Bristol, a member of the General Synod of the Church of England, and author of The Plausibility Problem: The Church and Same-Sex Attraction.*

QUESTIONS FOR REFLECTION

1. What are the dangers of forgetting the first sentence of this Article?
2. What are the dangers of forgetting the second sentence?
3. Are we as eager to remember the poor today as the Apostle Paul was in Galatians 2:10?

PRAYER

Our Gracious Lord Jesus Christ, though you were
rich, yet for our sake became poor, so that we by your
poverty might become rich: give to us such cheerful
and generous hearts that we in turn may give joyfully
to others from the blessings you have showered upon
us, storing up treasure for ourselves in heaven, for the
glory of your name. *Amen.*

Bible Reading

Matthew 5:33-37 and Jeremiah 4:1-2

Again you have heard that it was said to those of old, 'You shall not swear falsely, but shall perform to the Lord what you have sworn.' But I say to you, Do not take an oath at all, either by heaven, for it is the throne of God, or by the earth, for it is his footstool, or by Jerusalem, for it is the city of the great King. And do not take an oath by your head, for you cannot make one hair white or black. Let what you say be simply 'Yes' or 'No'; anything more than this comes from evil.

If you return, O Israel,
   declares the LORD,
   to me you should return.
If you remove your detestable things from my presence,
   and do not waver,
    and if you swear, 'As the LORD lives,'
   in truth, in justice, and in righteousness,
then nations shall bless themselves in him,
   and in him shall they glory.

Starter Question

Why does Jesus speak against vain and rash oath-taking?

Article XXXIX

OF A CHRISTIAN MAN'S OATH

~

As we confess that vain and rash Swearing
is forbidden Christian men by our Lord
Jesus Christ, and James his Apostle, so we
judge, that Christian Religion doth not
prohibit, but that a man may swear when
the Magistrate requireth, in a cause of faith
and charity, so it be done according to the
Prophet's teaching, in justice, judgement,
and truth.

Article xxxix

And so we come, if not precisely to the climax, certainly to the end of the Thirty-nine Articles, with this brief statement permitting the swearing of oaths in court. Oath swearing was an extremely significant feature of both political and spiritual realms in the sixteenth century. Indeed, it could be argued that the English Reformation as a whole was enacted through the swearing of oaths. The assent of the people to the will of the monarch was achieved by compelling them to swear oaths of loyalty and obedience.

By contrast, the continental Anabaptist movement had been teaching that all oaths were forbidden since the early part of the century. In his *Forty-Two Articles* (1552), Cranmer includes a number of Articles specifically directed against the teaching of the Anabaptists, several of which were discarded in the revised *Thirty-Nine Articles* (1563). As an aside, this is a reminder that all creeds and confessions are products of their historical context. Some of what was important in 1552 was already less relevant by 1563. The Article on swearing oaths, however, remained.

Permissible Oaths

'Vain and rash' swearing is forbidden, but in a case of law, adjudicated by a magistrate, Cranmer considers that it is permissible for

Christians to swear an oath. *The Heidelberg Catechism*, published in the same year as the Thirty-Nine Articles, takes a similar position:

> But may we swear an oath by the name of God in a godly manner? Yes, when the government demands it of its subjects, or when necessity requires it, in order to maintain and promote fidelity and truth, to God's glory and for our neighbour's good. Such oath-taking is based on God's word and was therefore rightly used by saints in the Old and the New Testament. (Q.101)

The biblical evidence is, as the catechism suggests, not as simple as reiterating Jesus' words in Matthew 5:33-37 and declaring all oaths forbidden. In the Old Testament, oaths were not merely permitted, they were at times commanded (e.g. Numbers 5:19). Even in the New Testament, Matthew 5 notwithstanding, Paul appears to make oaths, calling upon God as his witness, in 2 Corinthians 1:23 and Galatians 1:20. Hebrews 6:16 apparently commends the practice of swearing oaths.

As always in the Sermon on the Mount, Jesus argues from an existing understanding of the law to a greater one: 'You have heard it said... but I say to you.' In this case the existing understanding may be traced back to Leviticus 19:12 and Numbers 30:2. These verses prohibit false oaths and broken vows, but it seems that true oaths and kept vows are perfectly permissible. It was not the making of oaths which was forbidden, but the breaking of them.

Prohibited Oaths

However, Jesus pushes the case further, prohibiting any vows which invoke heaven, earth, Jerusalem or one's own head as the third-party participant. There are two reasons given: heaven and Jerusalem are forbidden because they are the throne of God and city of the great King, respectively. Swearing by one's own head is forbidden because it is beyond the oath-taker's control. Presumably swearing by the earth is forbidden for a similar reason.

In order to understand why these kinds of oaths are prohibited, it is helpful to analyse the very nature of an oath. Making an oath is a speech act which commits the speaker to the truth of his statement or the keeping of her promise *by invoking a third party as witness*. If the oath is unsuccessful, i.e. the statement is false, or the promise is broken, then the third party will be dishonoured and their own trustworthiness called into question.

The problem is: who or what is a suitable third party? The Anabaptists believed that Christians were not permitted to make oaths because there was no appropriate third party. How can we swear by things we can't control? And what can we control? Not even our own lives, let alone God or his heaven! So, they argued, we can make statements and promises, but we cannot invoke any third party. Rather, Christians should be truthful and trustworthy, and they should be known as such. Since oaths are normally only required when there is reason for doubt, there should normally be no need for Christians to use them.

Legal Oaths

However, Cranmer points out that there is a situation when oaths are required, not because of any reason to doubt the speaker but rather in the pursuit of justice and truth, in the cause of faith and charity. Oaths made in the legal setting of a court are not pointless oaths, which add nothing to the reliability of our words, nor rash promises which are easily made and easily broken. Oaths spoken in court legally and spiritually bind the speaker to their words, and to God as their witness. Such oaths are not to be taken lightly, since the consequences of breaking them are both temporal and spiritual. To break one's own word is a lie; to break an oath made in God's name is to make him a liar.

Honesty is a rare quality in this post-truth world. Keeping promises seems to be the exception rather than the rule. We don't need to swear by anything to keep our word and speak truth. Be the person who can be believed and trusted, whose yes is yes, and whose no is no (James 5:12). But if you are called to swear an oath, make sure to do so with the truthfulness and trustworthiness of God who is your witness.

Dr Ros Clarke *is the Associate Director of Church Society and editor of the Society's magazine, Crossway.*

QUESTIONS FOR REFLECTION

1. How do people in your culture assure you earnestly that they are telling the truth?
2. Why do people dislike those who 'spin' the truth and do not speak 'the truth the whole truth, and nothing but the truth'?
3. In a world of exaggerated claims and 'fake news' how can we ensure that our words are trustworthy and seen as such?

PRAYER

God of truth, for whom it is impossible to lie and whose word cannot be broken: bless us we pray with sincerity, integrity, and honesty of heart to speak the truth clearly and walk in the light, that we may not fall under condemnation with swindlers and the father of lies, through the merits of your Son, our Saviour Jesus Christ. *Amen.*

COMMENTARIES ON THE THIRTY-NINE ARTICLES

Various commentaries on the Articles are mentioned and quoted throughout this volume. Rather than filling the book with footnotes, the full details are given here so that readers can look up quotations as necessary, in the appropriate places.

E. J. Bicknell, *A Theological Introduction to the Thirty-nine Articles of the Church of England* (London: Longmans, Green and Co, 1919)

Gerald Bray, *The Faith We Confess: An Exposition of the 39 Articles* (London: Latimer Trust, 2009)

Martin Davie, *Our Inheritance of Faith: A Commentary on the Thirty Nine Articles* (Malton, North Yorkshire: Gilead Books Publishing, 2013)

W. H. Griffith Thomas, *The Principles of Theology: An Introduction to the Thirty-nine Articles* (London: Vine Books, 1930)

Oliver O'Donovan, *On the 39 Articles: A Conversation with Tudor Christianity* (Carlisle: Paternoster, 1986)

J. I. Packer and Roger Beckwith, *The Thirty-Nine Articles: Their Place and Use Today* (2nd Edition; London: Latimer Trust, 2006)

Scripture Index

Lightning Source UK Ltd.
Milton Keynes UK
UKHW010609100722
405623UK00001B/348